Social Perspectives in the 21st Century

Understanding Foucault For Beginners

SOCIAL PERSPECTIVES IN THE 21ST CENTURY

JASON L. POWELL - SERIES EDITOR

UNIVERSITY OF LIVERPOOL, UK

Foucault: Issues and Legacy
Jason L. Powell
2012. ISBN: 978-1-62257-539-8

Feminism
Jason L. Powell
2012. ISBN: 978-1-62257-540-4

Baudrillard and Postmodernism
Jason L. Powell
2012. ISBN: 978-1-62257-541-1

Habermas
Jason L. Powell
2012. ISBN: 978-1-62257-542-8

Understanding Foucault: For Beginners
Jason L. Powell
2013. ISBN: 978-1-62417-195-6

Understanding Power and Emotion: An Introduction
Jason L. Powell
2013. ISBN: 978-1-62417-200-7

Understanding Risk and Trust: A Short Conceptual Examination
Jason L. Powell
2013. ISBN: 978-1-62417-202-1

SOCIAL PERSPECTIVES IN THE 21ST CENTURY

UNDERSTANDING FOUCAULT

FOR BEGINNERS

JASON L. POWELL

New York

Copyright © 2013 by Nova Science Publishers, Inc.

All rights reserved. No part of this book may be reproduced, stored in a retrieval system or transmitted in any form or by any means: electronic, electrostatic, magnetic, tape, mechanical photocopying, recording or otherwise without the written permission of the Publisher.

For permission to use material from this book please contact us:
Telephone 631-231-7269; Fax 631-231-8175
Web Site: http://www.novapublishers.com

NOTICE TO THE READER

The Publisher has taken reasonable care in the preparation of this book, but makes no expressed or implied warranty of any kind and assumes no responsibility for any errors or omissions. No liability is assumed for incidental or consequential damages in connection with or arising out of information contained in this book. The Publisher shall not be liable for any special, consequential, or exemplary damages resulting, in whole or in part, from the readers' use of, or reliance upon, this material. Any parts of this book based on government reports are so indicated and copyright is claimed for those parts to the extent applicable to compilations of such works.

Independent verification should be sought for any data, advice or recommendations contained in this book. In addition, no responsibility is assumed by the publisher for any injury and/or damage to persons or property arising from any methods, products, instructions, ideas or otherwise contained in this publication.

This publication is designed to provide accurate and authoritative information with regard to the subject matter covered herein. It is sold with the clear understanding that the Publisher is not engaged in rendering legal or any other professional services. If legal or any other expert assistance is required, the services of a competent person should be sought. FROM A DECLARATION OF PARTICIPANTS JOINTLY ADOPTED BY A COMMITTEE OF THE AMERICAN BAR ASSOCIATION AND A COMMITTEE OF PUBLISHERS.

Additional color graphics may be available in the e-book version of this book.

Library of Congress Cataloging-in-Publication Data

Understanding Foucault : for beginners / editors, Jason L. Powell.
    p. cm.
 Includes bibliographical references and index.
 ISBN: 978-1-62417-195-6 (soft cover)
 1. Foucault, Michel, 1926-1984. 2. Social sciences--Philosophy. 3. Aging. 4. Social service. I. Powell, Jason L., 1971-
   B2430.F724U53 2013 194--dc23   2012040506

Published by Nova Science Publishers, Inc. † *New York*

CONTENTS

Chapter 1	Introduction	**1**
Chapter 2	Methods for Thinking	**5**
Chapter 3	The Making of the Modern Subject	**9**
Chapter 4	Implications	**17**
Chapter 5	Example 1 of a Foucauldian Approach: Aging and Prisons	**23**
Chapter 6	Example 2 of a Foucauldian Approach: Social Work	**33**
Chapter 7	Summary	**53**
References		**55**
Index		**65**

Chapter 1

INTRODUCTION

This text explores the major concepts of Michel Foucault. It is written at an introductory level with key examples illustrated. Michel Foucault was born on 15 October 1926 in Poitiers, France and died in June 1984. He was a French philosopher or more specifically a 'historian of systems of thought', a self-made title created when he was promoted to a new professorship at the prestigious Collège de France in 1970. Foucault is generally accepted as having been the most influential social theorist of the 20th century. He was also a French critical historian and became one of the most influential and controversial scholars of the post-World War II period. Foucault's project was to always deconstruct powerful discourses, which are in official social policies as 'empowering' to individuals, but Foucault argues such discourses legitimize the power of disciplines and professions but do not liberate people in wider society. His best-known works are *Discipline and Punish* (1977) and the multi-volume, but incomplete *The History of Sexuality* (1978). Foucault died of AIDS-related septicaemia in June 1984. Foucault has engendered an awareness that disciplines, institutions and social practices operate according to logics that are at variance with the humanist visions that are assumed to be culturally embedded (Powell and Biggs, 1999, 2000). In other words, the open meanings given to activities do not correspond to their overall consequences. Whether these outcomes are intended or accidental was less important to Foucault than the analysis of power. As Barry Smart (1983, 77) points out, Foucauldian analysis asks of power: 'how is it exercised; by what means?' and second, 'what are the effects of the exercise of power?' Within those strategies and tactics, investigation would need to be centred on the mechanisms, the 'technologies' employed and to the consequences of change.

One example of this disjuncture between humanist vision and cultural practices and its effects on the direction of modernity derives from Foucault's (1977) analysis of "utilitarianism". A pervasive theme of Foucault's work is the way in which the panopticon technique 'would make it possible for a single gaze to see everything perfectly' (1977, 173). Foucault describes how panopticism (based on the design of the utilitarian philosopher and social reformer Jeremy Bentham) becomes a process whereby certain mechanisms permeate social systems beyond actual, physical institutions. Techniques are thus 'broken down into flexible methods of control, which may be transferred and adapted ... (as)... centres of observation disseminated throughout society' (1977, 211-2).

The mechanisms used to extend the reach of centres of power through the social body will vary depending upon the grounds upon which they are required to operate. Their function is to evoke and sustain moral interpretations of particular social behaviours throughout intermittent observation such that their objects come to internalise their own surveillance around given norms of conduct. One important facet of Foucault's analysis of these processes is his preoccupation with historical periods in which conventional values are in flux as in the case of madness, discipline and sexuality (Foucault 1965, 1977 and 1978) and how the emergence of cultural discourses then inform commonsensical understandings of 'normality' (McNay, 1993). There are, in other words, periods in which particular sites and forms of conduct are subject to novel mechanisms and technologies in order to facilitate the transition from one state of affairs to another (Butler, 2000). These technologies may be overtly applied during periods of flux until moral relations have been accepted, whilst during the process of their application they both modify and are modified by the individuals or groupings charged with their implementation. Although Foucault does not impose any sense of causality on the development of such discourses, it is possible to discern the need for both an explicit moral reason and a method of operation, shaped to whatever new contexts are appropriate.

As Rouse (1994) has pointed out, an examination of the relationship between power and knowledge is central to interpreting and understanding social phenomena via a Foucauldian framework. One of the consequences of power and knowledge is that rather than the focus on the explicit use of a particular technique of knowledge by someone in power to cause a certain effect, attention is drawn to the reflexive relationship between both elements. This leads to a concern with: 'the epistemic context within which those bodies of knowledge become intelligible and authoritative. How statements were organised thematically, which of those statements counted as serious, who was empowered to speak seriously, and what questions and procedures were relevant to assess the credibility of those statements that were taken seriously. ...The types of objects in their domains were not already demarcated, but came into existence only contemporaneous with the discursive formations that made it possible to talk about them' (Rouse 1994: 93).

Just as knowledge shapes what action is possible and what power is exercised, those actions also shape the creation of new knowledge and what is thereby given credence. Over time, legitimate *'domains'* are established which both define what is real and what can be done about it. Other possible interpretations are simultaneously discounted and delegitimised. The result is a view and mode of practice in which power and knowledge support each other. These domains not only sustain, for example, certain professional discourses, they mould what those professions might become. This analysis of power and knowledge emphasises their entwinement and the processes that occur as a particular domain takes shape. It also marks a distinction between what a method for both understanding and obtaining knowledge produces and the relationship between the shaping of that product and the distribution of power.

How did Foucault proceed to 'uncovering' discourses and practices? An answer to this question requires an analysis of archaeology and genealogy and we turn to this in the next section of the chapter. It is important to examine these concepts as contextual backdrops for understanding his approach to subjectivity in the subsequent section, before finally moving on to consider the legacy of his work.

Chapter 2

METHODS FOR THINKING

ARCHAEOLOGY

It is through "historical investigation" that scholars can understand the present. However, when utilising historical inquiry, scholars should "use it, to deform it, to make it groan and protest" (Foucault 1980, 54). Foucault (1972; 1977) uses his methodological "tools" to disrupt history at the same time as giving history a power/knowledge re-configuration that makes his approach so distinctive and relevant to social theory and cultural analysis. In *The Archaeology of Knowledge* Foucault (1972) discusses "archaeology" as the analysis of a statement as it occurs in the historical archive. Further, archaeology "describes discourses as practices specified in the element of the archive" (1972, 131), the archive being "the general system of the formation and transformation of statements" (1972, 130). Whilst an understanding of language would ask what rules have provided for a particular statement, the analysis of discourse asks a different question: "how is it that one particular statement appeared rather than another?" (1972, 27).

The use of an archaeological method explores the networks of what is *said* and what can be *seen* in a set of social arrangements: in the conduct of an archaeology there is a visibility in "opening up" statements. Archaeology charts the relationship between statements and the visible and those 'institutions' which acquire authority and provide limits within which discursive objects may exist. In this approach we can see that the attempt to understand the relations between statements and visibility focuses on those set of statements that make up institutions such as prisons – instructions to prison officers, statements about time-tabling of activities for inmates and the structure and space of the carceral institution itself. This leads to the production of: 'a whole micro - penality of time (lateness, absences, interruptions of tasks), of activity (inattention, negligence, lack of zeal), of behaviour (impoliteness, disobedience), of speech (idle chatter, insolence), of the body (incorrect attitudes, irregular gestures, lack of cleanliness), of sexuality (impurity, indecency)' (Foucault 1977, 178). The crucial point is that this approach draws our attention to the dynamic inter-relationship between statements and institutions. Secondly, the attempt to describe "institutions" which acquire authority and provide limits within which discursive objects may act, focuses again on the institution which delimits the range of activities of discursive objects (Powell & Biggs, 2000) – it is at this point that an exploration of the architectural features of the institution would be used to understand spatial arrangements. In a similar context, Goffman (1968) wrote about how spatial arrangements of 'total institutions' operate to provide care and rehabilitation at an official level and capacity, underneath the surface. Such institutions curtail the rights of those within them: 'Many total institutions, most of the time, seem to function merely as storage dumps for inmates ... but they usually present themselves to the public as rational organizations designed consciously, through and through, as effective machines for producing a few officially avowed and officially approved ends' (Goffman 1968, 73). A Key difference between Goffman and Foucault's interpretations of institutions would be, however, that whereas Goffman sees total institutions as an aberration, untypical of society as a whole, Foucault's critique assumes that the carceral element of institutional life encapsulates a core feature of social life. A reason for wanting to study prisons, aside from its prior neglect, was: 'the idea of reactivating the project of a 'genealogy of morals', one which worked by tracing the lines of what one might call 'moral technologies'. In order to get a better understanding of what is punished and why, I wanted to ask the question: how does one punish?' (Foucault 1989, 276). Foucault never felt totally comfortable with archaeological analysis and felt that discourses did not reveal the irregularities between on going within social practices. As a result he developed his methodology during the course of his investigations.

GENEALOGY

Foucault acquired the concept of "genealogy" from the writings of Nietzsche. Genealogy still maintains elements of archaeology including the

Methods for Thinking

7

analysis of statements in the "archive" (Foucault 1977, 1980 and 1982). With genealogy Foucault (1977) added a concern with the analysis of power/knowledge which manifests itself in the "history of the present". As Rose (1984) points out, genealogy concerns itself with disreputable origins and "unpalatable functions". This can, for example, be seen in relation to psycho-casework, care management and probation practice (Biggs and Powell 1999, 2001; May 1991; 1994). As Foucault found in his exploration of psychiatric power: 'Couldn't the interweaving effects of power and knowledge be grasped with greater certainty in the case of a science as 'dubious' as psychiatry?' (1980, 109)

Genealogy also establishes itself from archaeology in it approach to discourse. Whereas archaeology provides a snapshot, a 'slice' through the discursive nexus, genealogy focuses on the processual aspects of the web of discourse – its ongoing character (Foucault, 1980). Foucault did attempt to make the difference between them explicit: 'If we were to characterise it in two terms, then 'archaeology' would be the appropriate methodology of this analysis of local discursiveness, and 'genealogy' would be the tactics whereby, on the basis of the descriptions of these local discursivities, the subjected knowledge's which were thus released would be brought into play' (Foucault 1980, 85).

Foucault is claiming that archaeology is a systematic method of investigating official statements such as dispostifs (McNay, 1994). Genealogy is a way of putting archaeology to *practical* effect, a way of linking it to cultural concerns: 'A genealogy of values, morality, asceticism, and knowledge will never confuse itself with a question for their 'origins' , will never neglect as inaccessible the vicissitudes of history. On the contrary, it will cultivate the details and accidents that accompany every beginning; it will be scrupulously attentive to their petty malice; it will await their emergence, once unmasked, as the face of the other. Wherever it is made to go, it will not be reticent – in 'excavating the depths', in allowing time for these elements to escape from a labyrinth where not truth had ever detained them. The genealogist needs history to dispel the chimeras of the origin, somewhat in the manner of the pious philosopher who needs a doctor to exorcise the shadow of his soul' (Foucault 1984, 80).

Chapter 3

THE MAKING OF THE MODERN SUBJECT

Foucault's use of genealogy cannot be divorced from an understanding of power, nor can the constitution of the subject. With this in mind our approach will be to consider his analytical ingenuity via an examination of different modes through which 'subjectivity' is constituted. Foucault (1982, 1983) grounded this as a pivotal mode of analysis that has been deployed in reflections on his own life (Miller, 1993). Subjectivity appears as both an experiential and discursive strategy that 'goes beyond theory' (Dreyfus and Rabinow 1983) and provides us with a way to problematise the explanatory value and relevance of his analyses.

We will discuss Foucault's approach to subjectivity in terms of classification, dividing and self-subjectification practices. These operate in ways to structure subjectivity under the auspices of the 'rise of modernity' where, commencing in the seventeenth century, the social sciences, early capitalism and institutions began to co-ordinate new ways of objectifying 'populations' in western societies. In Foucault's analysis the realm of the 'social' becomes the object of enquiry. Here, the term 'social' means: 'The entire range of methods which make the members of a society relatively safe from the effects of economic fluctuation by providing a certain security' (Donzelot 1980 p. xxvi). Thus, in Discipline and Punish, the study: 'traces the historical emergence of the social as a domain or field of inquiry and intervention, a space structured by a multiplicity of discourses emanating from the human sciences which, in their turn, are derived from, yet provide, a range of methods and techniques for regulating and ordering the social domain' (Smart 1983).

Foucault's (1980) main concern was to show that the 'truth' status of a knowledge derives from the field in which it, as a discourse, is employed and not from the interpretation of a subjects' thoughts or intentions. Discourses are powerful in that they operate as a set of rules informing thought and practice and the operation of these decides who or what is constituted as an object of knowledge. The relationship between the subject and truth should be viewed as an effect of knowledge itself. Quite simply, the subject is not the source of truth. As Foucault put it: 'what if understanding the relation of the subject to the truth, were just an effect of knowledge? What if understanding were a complex, multiple, non-individual formation, not `subjected to the subject', which produced effects of truth?' (Foucault in Elders 1974: 149).

Knowledge is not separate from the realm of `practice'. Knowledge is a practice that constitutes particular objects – non-theoretical elements – that are part of practice itself. Knowledge and the subject of knowledge are fused as part of the relationship between knowledge and power that is socially constructed: 'The important thing here, I believe, is that truth isn't outside power, or lacking in power: contrary to a myth whose history and functions would repay further study, truth isn't the reward of free spirits, the child of protracted solitude, nor the privilege of those who have succeeded in liberating themselves. Truth is a thing of this world: it is produced only by virtue of multiple forms of constraint. And it induces regular effects of power. Each society has its regime of truth, its `general politics' of truth' (Foucault 1980: 131)

Foucault is deliberately questioning the individual subjects' will to construct as he sets about exploring the relationship between 'discourse' and 'subjectivity'. What emerges is a grounded understanding of power/knowledge construction and reconstruction as discourses transform people into types of subjects - as classifying practices. Through these techniques of knowing, human attributes are studied, defined, organised and codified in accordance with the meta-categories of what is 'normal'. Classifying practices and techniques of normalisation designate both the objects to be known and the subjects who have the authority to speak about them. Discourses thus encompass both the objective and subjective conditions of human relations (1973, 232) and these emerging forms of social regulation, characterised by notions of discipline, surveillance and normalisation, are core to his theoretical studies (Foucault 1977).

The knowledge and practices are also referred to as 'epistemes' which are "the total set of relations that unite at a given period, the discursive practices that give rise to epistemological figures, sciences and formalised systems"

The Making of the Modern Subject

(Foucault 1972: 191). Social science disciplines, in different ways, order the status of those who can validate knowledge through inquiry. Foucault designates a discourse's function of dispersing subjects and objects as its 'enunciative modality' (Foucault 1972: 50). This modality encompasses roles and statuses and demarcated subject positions. Together they act to structure the space of regulation where the professionalisation of knowledge is instigated.

Dividing practices are deployed in order to maintain social order - to separate, categorise, normalise and institutionalise populations. In Madness and Civilization (1973a), Birth of the Clinic (1975) and Discipline and Punish (1977), Foucault illustrates how 'unproductive' people were identified as political problems with the 'rise of modernity'. The state divided these people into 'the mad', 'the poor' and 'the delinquent' and subsequently disciplined them in institutions: asylums, hospitals, prisons and schools (Foucault 1977). These exercises of disciplinary power were targeted at the subject and constituted techniques in these institutions. For instance, as we noted earlier, in Discipline and Punish Foucault argues that since the 18th century, prison authorities increasingly employed subtle regulatory methods of examination, training, time-tabling and surveillance of conduct on offenders in which we find a whole 'micro-penality'. Overall, dividing practices are seen as integral to the rationalism of the Enlightenment narratives of liberty, individuality and rights and as fusing with governmental forms of human calculation and audit.

The previous modes of classification and dividing practices co-exist. Professions examine, calculate and classify the groups that governments and institutions regulate, discipline and divide. The third mode of self-subjectification is more intangible. These practices designate the ways in which a person turns themselves into social subjects. Foucault claims that self-subjectification entails the deployment of technologies of the self: 'Techniques that permit individuals to affect, by their own means, a certain number of operations on their own bodies, their own souls, their own selves, modify themselves, and attain a certain state of perfection, happiness, purity, supernatural power' (Foucault, 1982: 10). In Foucault's work self-subjectification practices proliferate in the domain of sexuality because the occupying sciences of medicine, psychology and psychoanalysis obligate subjects to speak about their sexuality. In turn, these sciences characterise sexual identity as esoteric and dangerous (Foucault 1980). Thus, the association of sexual truth with self-subjectification gives 'experts' their power.

Self-subjectification practices inter-relate with classification and dividing practices to construct modern subjects. For instance, subjects are created by human sciences that classify problems, identities and experiences; the systems of power that divide, stratify and institutionalise types of 'elderly' subjects and the technologies of the self that impose upon individuals the reflexive means to problematise themselves. What Foucault seems to be confronting us with is a disturbing vision that our ideas about the depth of human experience are simply cultural veneers that exist in an interplay between power and knowledge. Shumway (1989) calls this a 'strategy of exteriority': a strategy that 'does not stem from a claim that the true being plain and visible, but from a rejection of the claim that the true is systematically disguised' (1989: 26). Foucault's analysis of subjectification practices highlight techniques used by administrative powers to problematise subjects and the games of truth employed by those who seek to know them through classification techniques..

Foucault juxtaposes his axis of classifying, dividing and self-subjectification practices with one that delineates three domains of subjectivity: the body, the population and the individual. These domains elaborate how modes of subjectivity traverse modern social relations.

THE BODY

The 'body' is a subject of discursive and political inscription. In Discipline and Punish Foucault (1977) claims that penal practices produce the 'soul' of the offender by disciplining the body and corporealising prison spaces. In prisons, the body's most essentialist needs - food, space, exercise, sleep, privacy, light and heat - become the materials upon which schedules, curfews, time-tables and micro-punishments are enacted. The body discipline developed in prisons has parallels throughout the broader disciplinary society. Indeed, the success of modernity's domination over efficient bodies in industry, docile bodies in prisons, patient bodies in clinical research and regimented bodies in schools and residential centres attest to Foucault's thesis that the human body is a highly adaptable terminus for the circulation of power relations.

It would be a mistake to believe Foucault is alone in arguing that the rule of the body is fundamental to modern politico-economical and professional regimes of power. Critiques of the domination of the body were the mainstay of Frankfurt theorists such as Adorno and Horkheimer (1944) long before Foucault's work. As he noted of their work: 'As far as I'm concerned, I think that the Frankfurt School set problems that are still being worked on. Among others, the effects of power that are connected to a rationality that has been

The Making of the Modern Subject

historically and geographically defined in the West, starting from the sixteenth century on. The West could never have attained the economic and cultural effects that are unique to it without the exercise of that specific form of rationality' (Foucault 1991, 117). Foucault's contribution, however, is to locate the ways in which 'bio-power' and disciplinary techniques construe the body as an object of knowledge. For example, The History of Sexuality depicts the dominion with which 19th century experts constructed a hierarchy of sexualised bodies and fragmented the population into groups of 'normal', 'deviant' and 'perverted'.

While Foucault's definition of the body has inspired numerous debates, the task of refinement and problematization have largely been the province of feminist scholars. Foucault has been criticised for his lack of sensitivity and attention to gender inequality and women's history thereby requiring theoretical revision in order to overcome such limitations (Powell and Biggs, 2000). Feminists have stressed that the body is both a site of regulation, where gendered identities are maintained and a site of resistance, where they are undone and challenged. McNay (1993) agrees with Foucault that 'sexuality is produced in the body in such a manner as to facilitate the regulation of social relations' (1993, 32). However, contra-Foucault, she notes that not all aspects of sexuality, corporeality and desire are products of power relations. Passionate social relationships based on friendship do not necessarily facilitate intense forms of surveillance and regulation. 'Friends' can transform disciplinary spaces and engage in disrupting practices. Similarly, Butler (1990, 140-141) claims that ritualised body performances that bind women to fictional feminine identities can also become deconstructive performances that expose the arbitrariness of identities.

THE POPULATION

Foucault outlines how the modern state enhanced its power by intervening in the very life of the 'bio-politics of the population' (1980, 139). Biopolitics leads to his overall perspective of politics or 'governmentality', "the art of government" (1991, 90). In this process power has two poles. First, a pole of transformation and second, the human body as an object of control and manipulation. The first revolves around the notion of 'scientific categorisation': for example, 'species' and 'population'. It is these categories that become object of systematic and sustained political intervention. The other pole of is not 'human species' but the human body: not in its biological sense, but as an object of control and manipulation. Collectively, Foucault calls these procedures "technologies" which centre around the 'objectification' of the body. The overall aim is to forge: 'a docile body that may be subjected, used, transformed and improved' (1977, 198).

Beginning with the inception of modernity, Western administrators rationalised their management of social problems with technically efficient means of population control: statistics, police, health regulations and centralised welfare. Such means constituted governmentality: an assemblage of ruling practices, knowledge authorities and moral imperatives that converged on the population in order to extend the reach of the state. The controversial point is that governmentality is more complex than state power. Custodial institutions and health programmes configured individuals into sub-strata of the population. For example, pension policies explicate 'the elderly' as a particular group of people, while statistics elaborate their status as a demographic entity (an 'ageing population'). Thus, the disciplinary formation of subjects as a population makes possible the government of subjectification.

THE INDIVIDUAL

If disciplinary gaze is a first step, then 'interiorization' of that gaze is the second. Foucault's social contructivism, consisting of classification and dividing practices, technologies of the self and political grids of bodies and populations has fuelled his critics claims that he deprives human subjectivity of agency (Smart 1983). Minson claims that Foucault burdens the body with being true subject of history and 'the flickering counterpart to the dull individual of sociology' (1985, 93).

Foucault emphasises two important aspects of individual agency that counteract his critics. First, the victims of modernity's disciplinary matrix - the prisoners, patients, and children - can subvert the regulatory forms of knowledge and subjectivity imposed upon them. Second, while power/knowledge relations construct governable individual subjects, such subjects are not fixed to their conditions of ruling and do become agents of resistance to them (Foucault 1977, 1991). To investigate the 'how' of power then requires: 'taking the forms of resistance against different forms of power as a starting point...it consists of using this resistance as a chemical catalyst so as to bring to light power relations, locate their position, find out their point of application and the methods used. Rather than analyzing power relations from the point of view of its internal rationality, it consists of analyzing power relations through the antagonism of strategies' (1982: 211). Power is exercised on free subjects and guides, but does not necessarily determine, conduct.

In this formulation the individual is not the traditional subject caught in a war between domination and liberation. Rather, the individual is the personal space where both active and passive aspects of human agency and identity surface in the context of material practices. The production of identity is implicated in the production of power which is both positive and negative. Identity may be imposed through the surveillance of a subject population. This surveillance produces both discipline (that is, conformity to the norm), and the disciplines (regulated fields of knowledge and expertise). Disciplinary surveillance involves first individualizing each member of the population to facilitate the collation of observations across the population.

From these observations, statistical norms are produced relating to a multitude of characteristics. These norms are then applied back to the subjected individuals who are categorized, evaluated and acted upon according to their relation to the produced norm. Foucault's work focused on the 'history of the present' and 'power/knowledge' synthesis and how the subject was formed (Foucault, 1977 and 1978). Here Foucault's work is on the 'microphysics of power' and the interplay of power relations, dividing practices and tactics in particular contexts (Foucault, 1977): the 'doctor' and 'patient'; 'prison officer' and 'prisoner'; 'teacher' and 'student' and 'care manager' and 'older consumer'.

Chapter 4

IMPLICATIONS

'It may be that the problem about the self does not have to do with discovering what it is, but maybe has to do with discovering that the self is nothing more than a correlate of technology built into our history' (Foucault 1993, 222).

Foucault's formulation presumes the notion that individual lives are never quite complete and finished – that in order to function socially individuals must somehow work on themselves to *turn* themselves into subjects. The notion of 'technologies' offers the opportunity for a particular analysis of the sites and methods whereby certain effects on the subject are brought about.

Objectifying technologies of control are, for example, those invented in conformity with the facets of self-understanding provided by criminality, sexuality, medicine and psychiatry investigated by Foucault. These are deployed within concrete institutional settings whose architecture testifies to the 'truth' of the objects they contain. Thus, the possibilities of self-experience on the part of the subject are in itself affected by the presence of someone who has the authority to decide that they are 'truly' ill such as a 'doctor' of medicine (Powell and Biggs, 2000). 'Subjectifying' technologies of self-control are those through which individuals: 'effect by their own means or with the help of others a certain number of operations on their own bodies and souls, thoughts, conduct and way of being, so as to transform themselves in order to attain a certain state of happiness, purity, wisdom, perfection or immortality' (Foucault 1988, 18).

The important issues that Foucault raises via a questioning of the centrality of the subject are associated to 'truthful' formulations of the task or the problem that certain domains of experience and activity pose for individuals themselves. The boundaries of self-experience change with every acquisition, on the part of individuals, of a possibility, or a right, or an obligation, to state a certain 'truth' about themselves. For example, bio-technology in popular culture can tell a 'truth' of selling a dream of unspoken desire of 'not growing old' to people. However, it is the self-experience of subjects that can refute, deny and accept the 'truth' claims of bio-technology. In the case of lifestyles in popular culture, the active adoption of particular consumer practices, such as uses of bio-technology contributes to a narrative that is compensatory in its construction of self (Biggs and Powell, 2001). Thus, the recourse to the notion of technologies of self is capable of accommodating the complexity of the 'subject'.

Although Foucault maintained the distinction between the technologies of power/domination and the technologies of self, these should not be regarded as acting in opposition to or in isolation to one another. Indeed, Foucault frequently spoke of the importance of considering the contingency of both in their interaction and interdependence, by identifying specific examples: 'the point where the technologies of domination of individuals over one another have recourse to processes by which the individual acts upon himself and, conversely, the points where the technologies of the self are integrated into structures of coercion' (Foucault 1993, 203). The distinction should therefore be considered as a heuristic device and not the portrayal of two conflicting sets of interests. Overall, we should see Foucault's entire works as providing ways of understanding social relations that require on our part active interpretation, not passive regurgitation.

To take one modern example of how we might think with, alongside (and against perhaps?) Foucault, take the question: how is modern bio-ethics rooted in a specific configuration of subjectivity? The body culturally represents the best hiding place, a hiding place of internal illnesses that remains inconspicuous until the advent of 'expert' intervention. In other words, what are the effects of this problematization given its conditions of possibility? Subjective relations to the self will be affected to the extent that social life confronts individuals with the proposition that this subjective truth – the truth of their relation to themselves and to others – may be revealed by 'bodies', which are also object of manipulation, transformation, desire and hope. In this way we might anticipate through 'culture' (Morris, 1998) the relations between illnesses, new technologies, power, the body and desire. While confronting an illness this involves a deliberate practice of self-transformation and such tranformativity must pass through learning about the self from the truth told by personal narratives within popular culture. How is this culture

Implications 19

and the body itself, however, interacting with and being changed by advances in bio-medical technology and the power of huge pharmaceutical companies?

Foucault is often seen as a structuralist, along with those such as Barthes, Althusser and Levi-Strauss. In reply to questions which sought to make such parallels, e was consistent: 'I am obliged to repeat it continually. I have never used any of the concept which can be considered characteristic of structuralism' (1989, 990. Perhaps the best way to view this is by examining his idea of historical 'events'. He refuses to see events as symptomatic of deeper social structures and focuses upon what seems to be marginal as indicative of relations of power. Events thereby differ in their capacity to produce effects. The following quote helps us see how this can be applied to cultural analysis: 'The problem is at once to distinguish among events, to differentiate the networks and levels to which they belong, and to reconstitute the lines along which they are connected and engender one another. From this follows a refusal of analyses couched in terms of the symbolic field or the domain of signifying structures, and a recourse to analyses in terms of the genealogy of relations of force, strategic development, and tactics. Here I believe one's point of reference should not be to the great model of language (langue) and signs, but to that of war and battle" (Foucault 1980, 114).

What about those questions concerned with whose culture, whose identity and how is this produced? These are the questions that pre-occupied Foucault. His refusal to see power as a property of say, a particular class, immediately leaves a question over his politics in terms of the idea of struggle? As he said: 'I label political everything that has to do with class struggle, and social everything that derives from and is a consequence of the class struggle, expressed in human relationships and in institutions' (1989, 104).

This leaves us with a question: against whom do we struggle if they are not the owners of power? Who creates cultures and how might alternative forms find public expression and does this change anything? These questions immediately bring forth issues concerning the relationship between Foucault and Marxist theory. Class structure, race and gender are key determinants of the position of individuals in capitalist society. It is difficult for 'techniques of resistance' to be mobilised when particular groups are de-commodified and marginalized and lose their social worth and voice (Biggs and Powell, 2001). At the same time Foucault sees subjectivity not as a fabricated part of a deeper reality waiting to be uncovered, but an aspect of the reality systematically formulated by resistances and discourses. He sidesteps the binary relationship set up by Marxist theory between true and false realities, ways of knowing and political consciousness (Foucault 1980) and seeks to loosen knowledge, ideas and subject positions from categories of social totality: for example, social formation, mode of production, economy and society.

Culture is rearticulated in Foucault's thought to historical and societal features ignored in those models of social reality that 'read off' culture according to deeper structures. Foucault looks to areas such as medicine, sexuality, welfare, selfhood and the law, and to marginalised social groups, local politics and the micro-levels of culture. In these studies he found social, discursive and historical substrata in which relations of domination were apparent that were not simply reducible to modes of economic exploitation. The idea of 'governing' then captures the ways in which the 'possible field of action of others' (Foucault 1982a: 221) are structured. Yet in inheriting this approach authors have produced panoptic visions in which resistance is subsumed within impersonal forces. This results from over-looking two main aspects in Foucault's work. First, in terms of his own question, what are the 'limits of appropriation' of discourse'? Without this in place, all does appear quiet on the battleground. Second, and relatedly, the agonism that exists between power and freedom (May 1999). This suggests that where there is power, there is also resistance; power thus presupposes a free subject. If there is no choice in actions, there is no power. A slave, therefore, is not in a power relationship, but one of physical constraint (Foucault 1982).

Foucault notes three types of struggle: those against domination; those against exploitation and those against subjection and submission. The latter, whilst rising in importance in the contemporary era, do not do so to the exclusion of domination and exploitation as many of his followers have appeared to suggest. To understand why particular actors enjoy more power than others, as opposed to seeing power as a 'machine in which everyone is caught' (Foucault 1980: 156), an account of resistance is needed. Because Foucault views freedom as part of the exercise of power, he does not provide for such an account. Yet, in answer to a question concerning 'power as evil', he spoke of the need to resist domination in everyday life: 'The problem is rather to know how you are to avoid these practices - where power cannot play and where it is not evil in itself' (Foucault 1991b: 18).

What makes Foucault's overall theoretical work inspiring, is how he animates and locates problems of knowledge as 'pieces' of the larger contest between modernity and its subjects. By downplaying the individual subject, Foucault shows how 'bodies' and 'populations' are sites were 'human beings are made subjects' by 'power/knowledge' practices (Smart, 1983, 44). To look for a possible form of trangression in order to change social relation, we must examine within contemporary arrangements the possibility for it to be

Implications 21

'otherwise'. We thus find, in Foucault's later work, an insistence upon the reversibility of discourses through 'resistance'. Subjects of power are also 'agents' who can strategically mobilise disjunctures in discourses and in so doing, open up the world of possibility in a world that seeks order through discipline and surveillance.

Chapter 5

EXAMPLE 1 OF A FOUCAULDIAN APPROACH: AGING AND PRISONS

This article provides a philosophical critique and analysis of the development and consolidation of prison officer power in the United Kingdom. It fundamentally questions the philosophical assumption that the role of the prison officer has evolved benevolently and independently, uncontested in their work and unbiased in their penal practices. Indeed, in the past fifteen years, penal policy in USA, UK and Australasia has focused on the management of prisoners with particular emphasis on the reform of the prison apparatuses (Woolf 1990). In the case of the UK, the process of Lord Woolf's report was imposed by central government backed up by appalling prison conditions (Sim 1992; Sim and Ryan 1996). Woolf's (1990) reforms offered the promise of greater autonomy for both prison workers and prisoners through the introduction of neo-liberal strategies of the 'social contract' and 'responsible prisoner' into policy areas traditionally directly controlled and subsidised by the U.K Home Office.

Indeed, the nature and fundamental principle of such prison provision for inmates has been the central cornerstone in debates within critical criminology in recent years. The continuing euphony of this question, and the powerful consciousness which it generates, is inextricably associated to the perceived role of the prison officer as a bulwark against an encroaching tide of criminality (Sim 1990). A distinctive feature of the prison system in the 1990s has been the systematic introduction of managerialism. Thus, John Clarke (1994) points not only to the substantial increase in the number of people working in welfare organisations with the title 'manager'; but also to the transformation of many formerly professionalised roles, into 'hybrids', where a significant aspect of the occupational identity is managerial. This is increasingly the case, for example, with head teachers, general practitioners, care managers and prison officers. Prison managerialism constitutes a move away from direct control towards 'monitoring' budgets associated with prison social relations. It was created as an economic solution looking for a social problem: prison life.

In the USA, UK and Australasia, the transition from a 'top down' penal policy that managed dependent prisoners to a neo-liberal politico state has gained momentum in recent years. Currently, social regulation and surveillance occur more 'bottom up': central control has been replaced by local power; management systems are inspired by consumer and markets models to prison life; and there is a reliance on risk assessment. Hence, at such a 'bottom up' level in the UK, prison managerialism is a technology put in place to promote social relationships of partnership and trust between professional prison officers and older prisoners.

Prison management is a technology aimed at transforming social relations within a mixed economy of prisons: public and private provision. The technology of prison management has become a space for the surveillance of prisoners. It is argued here that such a managerial mechanism is not of instigating trust, but is a technology for individual prisoner regulation and collective control. Hence, there are two dimensions which are particularly important to this paper. Firstly, there is the use of a Foucauldian perspective to locate the discontinuities in the relationship between professional power and older prisoners. Secondly, there is the question of power itself and its relevance to the emergence and consolidation of a discourse articulated by professional prison managers who assess, probe and inspect a distinct populational group: an 'elderly prison population'.

FOUCAULDIAN STUDIES

Michel Foucault's scholarly work has been acclaimed as 'the most important event in thought of our century' (Veyne 1984 quoted in Merquior 1985: 33). Throughout his work, he has attempted to develop perspectives on psychiatry, medicine, punishment and criminology.

Foucault (1977) has demonstrated (1996) the challenges to 'criminological disciplines' impinges upon the 'power/knowledge' axis. Crucially, such an axis permeates all formal and informal discourses, their language, logic, forms of domination and classification, measurement techniques and empiricism as essential elements in the technology of discipline and the process of normalisation. 'Professionals' such as prison officers are key interventionists in societal relations and in the management of social arrangements pursue a daunting power to classify with consequences for the reproduction of knowledge about 'prison' culture and simultaneous maintenance of power relations.

Yet whatever the quality and implications of professional agency, their recognition and legitimacy are rooted firmly in the determining contexts of 'structure' and their manifestation in the professional ideologies of control, regulation and power/knowledge (Powell 1998a). This article seeks to draw upon the insights of Foucault (1977). We critically engage with a number of sites of the disciplinary web of surveillance, power and normalisation and how these impact on both prison officers and older prisoners.

RE-APPLYING FOUCAULT TO POWER/KNOWLEDGE MANIFESTATIONS

Foucault's (1977) work has significance to the analysis of prison officers in two aspects. First, his analysis of punishment and discipline and medicine and madness has relevance to the experiences of prison life. Foucault describes how subjects of knowledge such as the stereotypical 'criminal' is constructed through disciplinary techniques, for example, the notion of the expert 'gaze' (1973: 29; 1977).

Secondly, Foucault (1977) makes it possible to analyse both the official discourses embodied in penal policies and those operating and implementing within the walls of prisons: prison officers and older prisoners:

> 'It was a matter of analysing, not behaviours or ideas, nor societies and their 'ideologies', but the problematizations through which being offers itself to be, necessarily, thought - and the practices on the basis of which these problematizations are formed' (Foucault 1980: 11).

The diverse works of Foucault (1967, 1976 and 1977) has problematised issues of madness and illness, deviance and criminality, and sexuality. These issues are conceptualised as socially constructed 'problems'. In these specific social issues, Foucault has problematised the role of the 'expert', social institutions, social practices and subjectivity that seem 'empowering' but are contingent socio-historical constructions and products of power and domination. The relevance to the power of prison officers is the recognition that social practices 'define a certain pattern of 'normalization" (Foucault 1977: 72). Such social practices are judged by 'experts' such as prison officers who problematise the behaviours of inmates. Prison officers are pivotal to Foucault's (1977) analysis of 'panoptic technology'. In addition, they probe and 'normalise judgement' on prisoners:

'The judges of normality are everywhere. We are in the society of the teacher-judge, the doctor-judge, the educator-judge, the 'social worker'-judge; it is on them that the universal reign of the normative is based; and each individual, wherever he may find himself, subjects to it his body, his gestures, his behaviour, his aptitudes, his achievements. The carceral network, in its compact or disseminated forms, with its systems of insertion, distribution, surveillance, observation, has been the greatest support, in modern society, of the normalizing power' (Foucault 1977: 304).

For Foucault (1977) 'normalizing power' involves the dimensions of physical and biological discourses and how these are inserted on the body. Both the aging prisoner and prison officer are located in a political field saturated with power relations which 'render [both prison officers and older prisoners as] docile and productive and thus politically and economically useful' (Smart 1985: 75). Hence, the prison officer plays a key role in such power relations as s/he takes responsibility for ensuring that older prisoners needs are regularly reviewed, resources are effectively managed.

POWER

The powerful role of the prison officer can be understood as a 'system of ordered procedures for the production, regulation, distribution, circulation and operation of statements' (Foucault 1980: 133). Furthermore, for Foucault (1980: 133) "truth' is linked in a circular relation with systems of power which produce and sustain it'. Here we can see his power/knowledge explication. All strategies that attempt to control prisoners involve the production and social construction of 'true' knowledge. Historically and before the prevalence of managerial prison systems, bio-medicine played a key role in articulating 'truths' about the social condition of older prisoners (Katz 1996).

The relevance of this to Foucault's work is the way in which the 'gaze' of truth constructs people as both subjects and objects of power and knowledge. In The Birth of the Clinic, Foucault illustrates how such a 'gaze' opened up 'a domain of clear visibility' (Foucault 1973: 105) for doctors for allowing them

Example 1 of a Foucauldian Approach   27

to construct an account of what was going on inside a patient, and to connect signs and symptoms with particular diseases. The space in which the gaze operated moved from the patient's home to the institution or the 'hospital'. This became the site for intensive surveillance, as well as the attainment of knowledge, the object of which was the body of patients. Both historically and contemporaneously, the identities of elderly people and old age have been constructed through expert discourses of 'decay' and 'deterioration' and the 'gaze' helps to intensify regulation over older people in order to normalise and provide treatment for such notions (Stott 1981; Foucault 1977; Katz 1996). Medical discourse, under the guise of science, was part of a disciplinary project orientated to:

> 'create a model individual, conducting his life according to the precepts of health, and creating a medicalized society in order to bring conditions of life and conduct in line with requirements of health' (Cousins and Hussain 1984: 151).

The way in which bio-medicine has interacted with other older people is a subtle aspect of control and power (Katz 1996). This legitimises the search within the individual for signs, for example, that s/he requires intense forms of surveillance and ultimately processes of medicalisation. This permeates an intervention into aging lives because practices of surveillance befit older people because of the pathological discourse permeation of 'its your age'. Surveillance of older people enabled bio-medicine to show 'concern' for their health and acquire knowledge about their condition. It, hence, constructs them as objects of power and knowledge:

'This form of power applies itself to immediate everyday life which categorises the individual, marks him by his own individuality, attaches him to his own identity, imposes a law of truth on him which he must recognise and which others have to recognise in him. It is a form of power which makes individuals subjects' (Foucault 1982: 212).

In general, medical power took its place alongside prison officer power in correcting, disciplining and normalising 'decaying' older prisoners. Nevertheless, the prison managerial gaze has come to rival the medical gaze. The power of the prison officer as an agent of control has supplemented medical power.

Prisons, Risk and Consumerism

Scientific dominance may have helped shape the construction of age identities, though it was not economical enough in its reach. Science has been bound up with 'risk' (Beck 1984) and what Giddens (1991) calls the process of 'reflexivity': this manifests because of the loss of faith in the exercise of scientific power/knowledge. The focus on risk has led to a situation in which 'science' has been slowly supplemented with financial discourses, and what we see, in relation to punishment, is an intensification towards management models and consumerism. Hence, the pervasive move to a 'mixed economy of punishment' has produced an extraordinarily powerful discourse and impacts upon treatment of older prisoners as 'consumers' that has come to accompany and supplement medical discourses of old age.

Indeed, the suspicion of scientific power/knowledge as manifested in 'bio-medicine' is mirrored by suspicions against welfare models as a means of finding a legitimised place for older people. The language of 'choice' to erode dependency has been colonised by both medical and health discourses. Indeed, the social regulation and surveillance of older prisoners can be seen as economically productive for central and local government. The Woolf Report (1990) centres upon a 'mixed economy of punishment' which highlights the incorporation of market forces to the construction and delivery of imprisonment (Ryan and Ward 1992). Hence, the mixed economy of punishment arguably fabricates representations of empowerment for older people. For example, many older prisoners needs have not been met due to power relations and ageism (Bytheway 1995; Powell 1998b). In this case, punishment provide schemes for the 'conduct of conduct' (Foucault 1976) dominated by power/knowledge and characterised by the discretionary autonomy of prison officers of the state. The relevance to older prisoners is that prison managerial power can intensify the ordering of aging identities through the processes of prison institutions and penal policies of the state. Hence, this evidence highlights the numbing consequences are 'docile bodies' (Foucault 1977) drained of empowered energy, reinforced by the attitudes of prison officers to aging that it is just that, 'your age', which requires an inspecting 'gaze' and assessment of needs from prison officers to older prisoners.

Coupled with this, Foucault's (1977, 1976) genealogical analyses of punishment and discipline and of sexuality, Foucault (1977) describes how 'techniques of surveillance' which occur in the 'local centres of power/knowledge' (for example, in the relationships between older people and care managers), have an individualising effect:

Example 1 of a Foucauldian Approach

'In a disciplinary regime...individualisation is 'descending'; as power becomes more anonymous and more functional, those on whom it is exercised tend to be more strongly individualised...In a system of discipline...(older people become more individualised than younger people)' (Foucault 1977: 193).

Techniques of surveillance are so calculated, efficient and specific that 'inspection functions ceaselessly. The gaze is everywhere' (1977: 195). Foucauldian ideas can identify two related mechanisms of surveillance: panopticism; normalisation and the probe of assessment. These mechanisms have helped shape and mould many of the experiences of older prisoners.

SURVEILLANCE AND OLD AGE

In Foucault's (1977) work 'Discipline and Punish', he presents the contrasting example between the execution of Damiens and the timetable of activities of 'young' offenders. The description of Damiens devastating and savage death serves to remind us of the strategy of torture upon the 'body' and the multiplicity of pains a body can endure. The timetable, by contrast, is specific, elaborate and a disciplinary technology which trains and organises individuals for their daily routines.

Foucault (1977) sees Jeremy Bentham's panoptican as the dominant example of disciplinary technology. For Foucault, the panopticon integrates power and knowledge, the control of the 'body' and the control of space into a technology of discipline. Bodies of people can be made productive and observable. Foucault remarks 'Is it surprising that prisons resemble factories, schools, barracks, hospitals, which all resemble prisons' (1977: 44). In the context of British punishment, prison life has a pre-occupation with monitoring and surveillance and this is crystallised in official discourse.

The perfect disciplinary apparatus, according to Foucault (1977: 173) 'would make it possible for a single gaze to see everything perfectly'. Foucault (1977) views the mechanism of panopticism as both efficient, since surveillance was everywhere and constant, and effective, because it was 'discreet', functioning 'permanently and in silence' (1977: 177). It also provides the scope for the supervision of those who were entrusted with the surveillance of others.

The technique of 'panopticism' was incorporated into prison relationships in the twentieth century so that older prisoners could be observed by professional power. Prison life for older people has elements of this kind of surveillance. Supervision is hierarchical in the sense that many older prisoners are accompanied by management discretionary power which embraces monitoring, assessing and calculating older people. Prison Wardens need to kept informed of progress of older prisoners in order to communicate this at formal review meetings to establish resource allocation to institutional spending planning. Surveillance of older prisoners does not stop at this point, as a network of reciprocal power relationships has been created:

> 'this network 'holds' the whole together and traverses it in its entirety with effects of power that derive from one another: supervisors, perpetually supervised' (Foucault 1977: 176-177).

Older prisoners who require services are the objects of scrutiny within society, but for such clients requiring financial services, the gaze reaches further. This evidences a strategic shift towards the policing of punishment and away from the post-war welfare consensus relationship to old age.

NORMALISING AGING

Foucault observes how the 'norm' entered social science disciplines by 'imposing new delimitations on them' (Foucault 1977: 184). While this standardised social science it also had an individualising effect 'by making it possible to measure gaps, to determine levels, to fix specialities and to render the differences useful by fitting them to one another' (1977: 185). This promoted the homogeneity of old age.

The identities of many older people are defined in relation to issues of abnormality and normality. The 'cut off' point were an old individual is or not deemed to be 'frail' is in no sense clearly defined and variations in levels of assessment is of increasing concern for prison managers. In a climate of resource constraints, distance from the norm has become valued amongst older prisoners who do not conform to discourses of 'slow' and 'deterioration' (Katz 1996).

The process of observation objectifies particular older prisoners as 'diagnoses began to be made of normality and abnormality and of the appropriate procedures to achieve... to the norm' (Smart 1985: 93). In this way studying and examining the body and mind of older people was and is intrinsic to the development of power relationships:

Example 1 of a Foucauldian Approach 31

'the examination is at the centre of the procedures that constitute the individual as effect and object of power, as effect and object of knowledge. It is the examination which ... assures the great disciplinary functions of distribution and classification' (Rabinow 1984: 204).

The 'probing' technique, argues Foucault, combines panopticism and normalisation and 'establishes over individuals a visibility through which one differentiates them and judges them' (Foucault 1984: 184). The 'assessment' is a function of a disciplinary technique. Foucault (1977) argues an individual is established as a 'case' and may be 'described, judged, measured, compared with others, in his very individuality. This individual may also have to be trained or corrected, classified, normalised, excluded' (Foucault 1977: 191).

Foucault (1977) sees the 'assessment' as central a technique that renders an individual an object of power/knowledge. In the assessment leading the opening for medical services, the statement of an 'aging body' is established in relation to normalised standards of rights and risks. Thus, older prisoner will be probed for social, psychological and economic factors such as 'frailty', 'financial resources' and expected levels of 'supervision'. This probe of assessment:

'indicates the appearance of a new modality of power in which each individual receives as his status his own individuality, and in which he is linked by his status to the features, the measurements, the gaps, the 'marks' that characterise him and makes him a 'case' (Foucault 1977: 192).

Following a prison medical assessment, certain aging identities are marked out for surveillance throughout the remainder of his/her sentence. Prison officers also come under the scrutiny of the continuous review of older prisoners needs. All are caught by a gaze which is 'always receptive' (Foucault 1977: 89) and the very existence of the discourse of 'frailty' provides a further rationale for the control of the 'elderly population' in prisons.

CONCLUSION

This paper has problematized the explanatory insights from Foucauldian theory and philosophy. Once older prisoners are established as a socially significant object of power/knowledge, prison managerial techniques deem it necessary find the 'truth' about their needs, to analyse, describe and to understand. The focus towards issues of elder abuse in prisons takes place in a process in which attention is being directed towards individual bodies and control of 'aging populations'. The aging prisoner is part of a machinery of power, a power that creates the body, isolates it, explores it, breaks it down and re-arranges it. A knowledge of the aging body therefore requires a mechanism of discipline, that is, a machinery of power that is part of the managerial production of knowledge (Powell 1998). Discipline was the 'political anatomy of detail' (Armstrong 1983), that is to say older prisoners become known and understood as a series of useable bodies which could be manipulated, trained, corrected, controlled and to legitimise managerial professions. The outcome in relation to imprisonment is a cumulation of increasingly detailed observations that simultaneously and inescapably produce knowledge of older prisoners.

Chapter 6

EXAMPLE 2 OF A FOUCAULDIAN APPROACH: SOCIAL WORK

This chapter explores the relevance of a Foucauldian approach to a second example, namely, social work. In terms of social welfare, itself a discourse, clients or service users and social workers would need not simply to follow the rules that legitimize what they can say and do, but also to work on themselves so each can become the sort of person who can be seen and heard within that discourse. If they are not careful, both professionals and users of health and welfare systems become trapped in a dance of mutually maintained positions that serves to sustain a particular view of the world and the remedies, the technologies that can be brought to bear on it. An analysis of power, which follows the Foucauldian pathway as outlined above, must examine at least three aspects of how such power is created and maintained. First, the analysis must examine the genealogy of existing relations, how they have emerged, and the discourses they reflect and reinforce. Secondly, attention must be given to the distribution of power and knowledge that these relations imply. Finally, technologies of welfare such as psychosocial casework and case management will need to be critically assessed as approaches to the self that hold certain webs of power in place. Each will contribute to the ways in which subjects enmeshed in certain relations apply techniques of identity control to themselves. For Foucault (1977) power is a concept often discussed as fundamental to the relationship between professionals and the society in which they operate but one rarely conceptualized as the product and producer of such relationships. For example, his analysis of power offers a set of strategies (Foucault, 1977, 1978) for understanding how discourse produced within a network of disciplinary activities and embedded in social policy constructs social workers' experiences and their identities, as well as the experiences and identities of those with whom they interact. At the same time, the dynamics of these relationships reinforce and modify the discourse that made such meaning possible in the first place.

Bryan Turner (1997) argues that Foucault's contribution to the analysis of power is important in three ways as it provides: (i) analysis of the relationship between power and knowledge; (ii) the emergence of the modern self through disciplinary technologies; and (iii) analysis of governmentality. Central to Foucauldian analysis is discourse, inseparable combinations of knowledge and power that along with their respective technologies – specific techniques and associated practices, i.e., assessment and care planning – operate to subjugate individuals in specific circulations or 'regimes of power'.

Foucault proposes that since the 17th century a particularly modern form of power has developed, 'bio-politics', a politics of the population that operates through two modalities, 'totalizing' and 'individualizing', producing a two-way process between the subject as a private individual and the subject as a public citizen (Miller, 1993). Foucault rejects claims that any particular group or class have a monopoly over power; rather, power circulates via a myriad of social networks penetrating deep into the far corners of social life playing out its effects through the everyday interactions of autonomous individuals. Power and knowledge combine in disciplinary processes that act on the body producing the modern subject as docile, productive and willing to participate in their own management (Foucault, 1977). Through these processes, power operates to differentiate groups of people and individuals from other individuals, finally producing the components of individual subjectivity.

Foucault uses the idea of 'resistance' to describe how the effects of power may be only partially successful in specific social contexts enabling challenges to and changes in existing power relations (Nettleton, 1997). This occurs in a number of ways but is located with two forms of possibility. First, the reemergence of 'popular knowledges', the historical contents of conflict and struggle that have become submerged under a veneer of functionalist coherence and order; and second 'insurrections of subjugated knowledges', knowledges disqualified as inadequate, unscientific or lacking sophistication. In both these possibilities, we can see the possibility of a range of accounts, that is, professionals alienated from practice, oppressed communities, and the disadvantaged and disenfranchised.

In this formulation, Foucault (1977) departs from many conceptualizations of power by suggesting that power in itself is 'relational' (Parton, 1994).

Therefore, whilst one social actor may exercise power interacting with other individuals, we also need to be aware that all other individuals also exercise 'power' in their social relationships often expressed through 'resistance' in its dance with surveillance. The outcome is to produce a dialectical relationship between knowledge, power and action that is productive in the sense of creating particular possibilities but which also maintains a level of uncertainty and unpredictability in terms of actions, providing opportunity for the exercise of discretion.

In relation to the modern self, Foucault (1977) identifies three key processes in the objectification of individuals. Hierarchical observation, the development of ever-sophisticated processes of surveillance (often discussed as 'panopticon' or the 'gaze') that are constantly but unobtrusively maintained engulfing all in a web of watching. Normalizing judgements, the production of classification systems that enable the identification of 'norms' of social functioning that allow ongoing comparison of individuals enabling small transgressions to become the focus of disciplinary attention and the examination. The latter brings together the two former elements linking specific knowledges with particular practices in the exercise of power while engaging experts – professionals – in a network of writing and documentary accumulation that identifies individuals as deserving or risky, noting individual features, specifying appropriate interventions and recording progress. Documentation fixes the objectification of individuals in writing codifying, calculating difference and drawing comparison and embedding this in discourse, i.e., 'evidence based practice' which, in turn, disciplines and regulates professional activity. However, rather than the objectifying processes discussed above, Foucault's (1977) concept of 'subjectification' involves a range of 'technologies of the self' where individuals engage with processes Foucault likens to the confessional. Individuals, incited by discourse, engage in reflective processes where they speak the truth about themselves, gain self-knowledge, and then act on that self-knowledge in an ethic of self-formation producing the self-managing individual central to neo-liberal rule (Dreyfus and Rabinow, 1982; Miller, 1993; Turner, 1997).

GOVERNMENTALITY

Foucault's concept of governmentality enables analysis of the processes, techniques, and procedures that produce the moral regulation of the choices of autonomous individuals (Miller, 1993; Osborne, 1997; Rose, 1993, 1996).

Since this is a feature of the very core of contemporary social policy, it enables us to identify ways in which discourse constitutes categories of identity, regulating morals, and directing life choices. Such processes of ethical self-formation give rise to a core feature of neoliberal forms of government, the government of the self by the self. Discourse operates through a myriad of statutory and non-statutory social institutions, such as citizen associations, charities, trade unions, families, schools, hospitals, and workplaces that have no direct political affiliations and diverse histories. Foucault's (1978) conceptual tool of 'governmentality' is the means through which neoliberal modes of government afford expertise a key role and function in the management of individual and collective conduct. However, this role differs markedly from that afforded professionals under former regimes as neoliberal government, which 'seeks to detach the substantive authority of expertise from the apparatus of political rule, relocating experts within a market governed by the rationalities of competition, accountability and consumer demand' (Rose, 1993: 285). Rather than being the territory of direct interventions, government instead becomes the structuring and regulation of potential choices of autonomous individuals with expertise operating in a semi-autonomous relationship with the state (Miller, 1993). This has had an impact on the professional changes in social work.

BIO-POLITICS

Foucault (1977: 87) outlines how the modern state enhanced its power by intervening in the very life of the 'bio-politics of the population'. Bio-politics leads to his overall perspective of politics or 'governmentality', 'the art of government' (Foucault, 1991: 90). In this process power has two poles. First, a pole of transformation and, secondly, the human body as an object of control and manipulation. The first revolves around the notion of 'scientific categorisation', for example, 'species' and 'population'. It is these categories that become object of systematic and sustained political intervention. The other pole of is not 'human species' but the human body: not in its biological sense, but as an object of control and manipulation. Collectively, Foucault (1977: 198) calls these procedures 'technologies' which centre round the 'objectification' of the body. The overall aim is to forge 'a docile body that may be subjected, used, transformed and improved'. Beginning with the inception of modernity, Western administrators rationalised their management of social problems with technically efficient means of population control:

Example 2 of a Foucauldian Approach 37

statistics, police, health regulations and centralised welfare. Such means constituted governmentality: an assemblage of ruling practices, knowledge authorities and moral imperatives that converged on the population in order to extend the reach of the state. The controversial point is that governmentality is more complex than state power. Custodial institutions and health programmes configured individuals into substrata of the population. For example, pension policies explicate 'the elderly' as a particular group of people, while statistics elaborate their status as a demographic entity (an 'ageing population'). Thus, the disciplinary formation of subjects as a population makes possible the government of subjectification.

RELEVANCE FOR SOCIAL WORK

Despite ongoing pressures, professional power persists as a foundational element in the management of the population. On the one hand, professional *surveillance* restricts practice while on the other complexity opens the space for *resistance* and new formulations of power relations. This has important implications for how vulnerable groups are at risk. Foucault's ideas have been used to understand the construction of social welfare, particularly through the lens of governmentality seen to be at work in the intense process of rationalization of modern social work over the past 20 years in the United Kingdom, Canada, Australia, and North America. In the UK, most pressing have been concerns identified with the degeneration of the social democratic accord (Clarke and Newman, 1997; Harris, 2002), as it gave way to new priorities produced by the neoliberal consensus that has emerged since the 1980s. This has seen 'New Labour' governments – between 1997 and 2010 – extend the project of restructuring the relationship between the state and its citizens initiated by New Right Conservatives (Jordan, 2005). Social services, once envisaged as the province of a universal citizenship, are now mere supports for the irresponsible (Butler and Drakeford, 2001; Harris, 2002). The state, once the principle focus for analysis, now appears as merely one among a range of contextually and historically specific elements within multiple circuits of power (Rose, 1999). A Foucauldian analysis identifies the assemblage of ruling practices, knowledge authorities, and moral imperatives, which converge on social work in order to govern the conduct of social workers and those they aim to support (Rose and Miller, 1992; Parton, 1994; Rose, 1996; 1999). In this formulation, differences between the government of populations and management of conduct in specific localized spaces are technical rather than ontological. Social policy, enacted via a range of institutions, such as schools, universities, hospitals, and workplaces, aims to act on the 'well-being' of the population as a whole promoting social cohesion while simultaneously influencing the innumerable decisions taken by individuals in their everyday lives thus managing their conduct (Rose, 1999). This section considers the changing context of contemporary social work in England before moving on to an application of Foucault's ideas to professional practice focusing on two areas: surveillance and social work and discretion and power.

MODERN SOCIAL WORK IN ENGLAND

Over the past five years, new policy frameworks covering children and adults have emerged in England, including *Every Child Matters* (UK Department of Health, 2003), *Independence, Well Being and Choice* (UK Department of Health, 2005a), *Choosing Health* (UK Department of Health, 2005b), *Our Health, Our Care, Our Say* (UK Department of Health, 2006), and *Putting People First* (HM Government, 2007). These policies have profoundly restructured the terrain of social work, social care, education, and health management in England. At the macro-level, this framework – bio-politics – targets the population with notions of 'well-being' articulated with discourses of social inclusion, participation, and responsibility. At the micro-level its effects work by managing individual conduct inciting individuals to seek 'well-being' by balancing choices between the often-contradictory imperatives of the 'market' with those of individual and collective obligation (Rose, 1999), thus establishing the basis for moral self-regulation mirrored in a myriad of formal and informal social contexts (Miller, 1993).

This formula is not merely rhetorical. Organizational structures across a range of social institutions, including personal social services, reflect similar logic. The introduction of quasi-markets in social services separated functions previously held within unified departments dividing assessment of need from the provision of support; the latter devolved to an increasing range of semi-autonomous organizations in the third sector (Clarke and Newman, 1997). In conjunction, government acts indirectly on these autonomous organizations identifying budgets, setting targets, and regulating activity. In return, those individual organizations that enter into government contracts act reflexively and demonstrate effective self-management (Rose, 1999). As part of this, the role of social workers within these contracted organizations is shaped by

Example 2 of a Foucauldian Approach

increasing managerialist demands for information, particularly in response to audit and risk assessment (Parrot and Madoc-Jones, 2008) leading to claims of increased chapterwork and a corresponding demise of face-to-face work (Jones, 2001; Lewis and Glennerster, 1996; Pithouse, 1998; Postle, 2001; Sheppard, 1995).

This new policy framework added another dimension to the increasingly dispersed context of social care by effectively dividing provision for children and families from provision for adults. This has been compounded more recently by demands for specialization in prequalifying social work training (Laming, 2009), the former leaving some to comment that developments represent the final nail in the coffin of the unified social work department envisaged by Seebohm (Garrett, 2002). In addition, lead roles, once clearly the province of social services, are now set within a complex array of relationships between statutory and non-statutory organizations, including a range of service-user and consumer groups. Such relations often reflect power relationships at a more local level, highlighting Foucault's emphasis on the importance of micro-politics (Gordon, 1980) which, in the process, produce an increasingly diverse range of roles for social workers operating in the different segments of welfare or social care. In addition, a whole plethora of new roles has emerged, e.g., personal advisors in Connexions service, which have chipped away at the traditional bases of the social work role. At the same time, information and communication technologies have provided novel spaces for organizing meaning (Salvo, 2004), effectively structuring activities like assessment and establishing modern opportunities for the surveillance of workers and service users (Garrett, 2002, 2005), while also providing innovative possibilities for representing the disadvantaged.

Notwithstanding clear differences in the power and prestige of so-called 'caring professions' (Hugman, 1991), traditional professions, such as medicine, as well as newer and less established 'quasi-professions', such as social work, have been considered more resistant to, or even immune from, broader economic and political power (Leonard 1997). Reasons for this assumption have differed, but in general the profession's reliance upon knowledge and technical skill for practice, as well as internally restricted access and an extensive period of academic training, has allowed employee discretion and control to prevail (Johnston, 1972). However, critics have challenged this orthodox view noting the extent to which professions have always tended to adapt readily to forces of change, as well as conform to organizational policies and procedures (Brint, 1994; Johnson, 2001). For example, the expansion of managerialism has significantly reduced professional discretion (Baines, 2004; Jones, 2001). Despite this, it is questionable the extent to which professional practice has been seriously challenged by resistance arising from a resurgence of popular or subjugated service user knowledges (Chambon, 1999).

Hence, a Foucauldian approach to the social work profession (Biggs and Powell, 2001; Fournier, 1999, 2000, 2001) attempts to integrate the micro-political tactics of professionalization within a broader network of power relations through the analysis of discourse and regimes of power/knowledge. For Foucault, professionalism in itself is 'a disciplinary mechanism', which associates specific practices with particular worker identities, professional knowledge, and rules of conduct thus legitimizing professional authority and activity. In turn, these norms act as a form of *discipline* over otherwise autonomous professional power-regulating behaviour through self-management (Fournier, 1999). Thus induction into professions, in terms of *both* knowledge *and* conduct, serves to construct a specifically governable subjectivity rooted in self-disciplinary mechanisms, such as reflective practice and models of supervision (Gilbert, 2001; Grey, 1998). Therefore, the political proximity of welfare professions to the apparatus of government can be described as follows: 'professionals are both the instrument and the subject of government, the governor and the governed' (Fournier, 1999: 285).

Paradoxically, professional autonomy, particularly in areas such as social work, is the reason why the professions remain necessary, due to their ability to manage complex and unpredictable situations, and the focus for the deployment of a range of disciplinary technologies that produce patterns of accountability targeting, limiting, and controlling the exercise of autonomy (Rose, 1999). Indeed, Biggs and Powell (2001: 99) warn:

> In terms of social welfare, itself a discourse, both clients and social workers would need not simply to follow the rules that legitimise what they can say and do, but also to work on themselves in order to become the sort of person who can be seen and heard within that discourse. If they are not careful, both professionals and users of health and welfare systems become trapped in a dance of mutually maintained positions that serves to sustain a particular view of the world and the remedies, the technologies, that can be brought to bear on it.

This view of welfare professions as modes of disciplinary control also provides a useful counterbalance to critical perspectives, which reinforce stereotypes of pampered and privileged professionalism. In recasting professionalism as a source of influence and status concomitant with self-discipline and controlled performance, the Foucauldian position also links professionals with a wider range of control strategies (Dyer and Keller-Cohen, 2000; Fleming, 2005; Hochschild, 1983; Whitehead, 1998). This places professional expertise at the heart of disciplinary technologies designed for the management of populations.

IMPLICATIONS FOR SOCIAL WORK PRACTICE

Social Work and Surveillance

This section extends this Foucauldian analysis by focusing on two contemporary issues faced by social work practitioners, both of which involve different technologies of surveillance. The first concerns systems of knowledge provided by information and communications technologies (ICT), which shape social work activity while the second considers that archetypal proviso for professional autonomy, the exercise of discretion. Together these two pillars of contemporary practice demonstrate all three elements of what Foucault (1977) describes as discipline: hierarchical observation, normalizing judgments, and the examination. For example, the clients of social work practice and social workers' themselves are seen as both object and subject subjugated to ever more sophisticated modes of surveillance while paradoxically creating spaces for innovation and resistance. In the case of the former, the objectifying effect of audit exploits electronic capabilities for surveillance (Garrett, 2005; Rose, 1999), while the latter retains the familiar professional technologies of supervision promoting self-reflexive surveillance (Gilbert, 2001; Rose, 1996, 1999).

Indeed, one of the key issues in health and social care, where a Foucauldian approach illuminates its microphysics of power, can be situated within an exemplar of information and communication technologies. Salvo (2004: 43) describes 'communication and information systems' as the art, science, and business of organizing information so that it makes sense to people who use it while also highlighting its democratizing potential theoretically promoted by participation. However, in practice, data protection and freedom of information legislation circumscribe these technologies promoting a potentially contradictory position that simultaneously enables and restricts access to information. In UK health and social services, this tension demands adherence to the 'Caldicott standard' (Richardson and Asthana, 2006; UK Department of Health, 2002). Salvo (2004) also highlights the potential of such technologies as 'professional space' promoting what he describes as 'critical action' which also opens up the possibility of innovation and resistance as workers exploit the totalizing effects of such processes. Similarly, Parrot and Madoc-Jones (2008) explore the potential of ICT for resistance, the exercise of discretion, and the development of new forms of social work practice.

Nevertheless, information and communications technologies increasingly order the practice of a range of professionals, including social workers, subsuming in the process older chapter-based standardized assessment and associated needs focused processes. Garrett (2002, 2005) notes the pervasiveness of such technologies across the public sector, thus ensuring that it is impossible to avoid engaging with these technologies at some level, the implication being that adopting a stance of 'refusing to participate' is not a serious option (Freenberg, 1991), although resistance and subversion are always possibilities (Fleming, 2005).

Information and communication technology is a core element of policy and central to strategies for governing social welfare often located within the rhetoric of 'joined up government' and influenced by the private sector (Garrett, 2005; Hudson, 2000a, 2000b; Selwyn, 2002). Parallel rhetoric of 'shared assessment processes' recruit both the service user and a range of professionals in statutory and non-statutory agencies to 'data sharing' supported by such technologies. At the same time, a variety of management information systems enable the passing of performance data between localized and centralized levels of government linking the two poles of bio-politics.

The significance of these systems from a Foucauldian perspective is twofold. First, they engulf all in architectural labyrinth of information, a form of panopticon establishing a level of surveillance of social workers and service users, constantly monitored through electronic forms of audit. Secondly, they institutionalize particular discourses in the very operation of the system through the nature and types of questions asked. Garrett (2005: 453) notes the *'narrow, normative and prescriptive view'* embedded in a range of assessment tools promoted by government agencies observing that:

> Social work is increasingly being ordered, devised and structured by academics, policy makers and e-technicians far removed from the day-to-day encounters, which practitioners have with the users of services. This is reflected in the emerging software architecture and in the greater use of centrally devised e-assessment templates which attempt to map contours of social work engagements and which construct new 'workflows'(Garrett, 2005: 545).

Example 2 of a Foucauldian Approach 43

In England, guidelines related to community care policy (UK Department of Health and Social Services, 1990; UK Department of Health, 2005b, 2006) provide familiar strategies of identification, assessment, care planning, care packages, monitoring, and review. However, subtle changes in the rationalized deployment of this technology shifted its focus away from support for clients toward surveillance and monitoring. A new language of audit concerned with 'outcomes' and 'risk' shaped social work activity in child care and community care producing particular expectations (D'Cruz et al., 2009; Rose, 1999). Monroe (2004) notes positive and negative consequences of this development but, in a similar vein to Garrett (2005), observes the involvement of external inspectorates, such as the Audit Commission and the Social Services Inspectorate alongside senior managers in setting goals and an absence of practising social workers. Positive developments include increased accountability and standardization of social work practice. However, this may be at the cost of producing a punitive environment and reducing social work to a simplistic description of practice that operates within a culture of blame and protocolization.

Furthermore, in the context of child welfare, Tilbury (2004) notes how the values implicit in performance indicators provide a narrow conception of child welfare that overstates regulatory concerns while underplaying the importance of supporting families to provide safe care at home. Likewise, Garrett (2003: 443) observes that the:

> Framework for Assessment of Children in Need and their Families (DH/DfEE/HO, 2000), contains a preoccupation with the ecological approach and the use of questionnaires and scales that produces social work as a reactive activity narrowly focused on child abuse at the expense of proactive family support services.

This 'narrow, normative and prescriptive view' has particular consequences for some targets of policy due to what Booth et al. (2006) describe as 'temporal discrimination'. Discussing the experience of child protection procedures by parents with intellectual disabilities, they note how the prevailing wisdom in policy and practice over avoiding delays and the tendency for time-limited interventions works against people with poor conceptions of time and related skills. They argue that 'tick box' social work reliant on systems and procedures has replaced analysis and judgment to the detriment of some of the most vulnerable of social workers' clients. This provides a new tactic for the surveillance of contemporary social work that can best be described as 'time discipline' (Garrett, 2003), reflecting Jones's (2001) observation that tactics first used to constrain the autonomy of radical social workers now targets mainstream practitioners. Processes of protocolization, the time spent on activities like chapterwork – or electronic form filling – has particular relevance for a Foucauldian analysis of social work, as power relations embedded in routinization can 'define a certain pattern of 'normalization': 'The carceral network, in its compact or disseminated forms, with its systems of insertion, distribution, surveillance, observation, has been the greatest support, in modern society, of the normalizing power' (Foucault, 1977: 304).

Keenan (2001) observes similar phenomena in the USA related to compulsory documentation and recording for users of mental health services. She describes the constricted, objectifying image of service users provided by the assessment and monitoring processes informed by the normalizing and medicalized discourses of mental health embedded in *The Diagnostic and Statistical Manual of Mental Disorders* (DSM-IV-TR) (American Psychiatric Association, 1994), which defines healthy behaviours in relation to particular norms and in opposition to unhealthy or forbidden behaviours. At the same time, she uses Foucauldian insights to identify how the 'gaze' of diagnosis makes the service user visible while shading the powerful and privileged.

In a similar vein, Scheyett (2006) agues that discourses of evidence- based practice effectively silence the service user and the practitioner. This occurs as the dialogue between service users and practitioners over experiences and knowledge of the 'real world' become subjugated to disciplinary knowledge external to this dialogue which, through its status as truth, discredits alternative conceptions of events and their meanings (Foucault, 1978) as tactics of government, information technologies objectify and render visible but in the same movement silence the targets of policy. As Heffernan (2006) notes, the language of user involvement dispersed throughout social policy has enabled government to narrow the range of options available.

Social work clients are not the only targets of the discourses carried by this information infrastructure. The rights of carers to have their needs assessed has valorized caring and carers in a way that 'may squeeze out the last remnants of the right not to care' (Harris, 2002: 272) thus reinforcing a particular ethical gaze within objectified and electronic formats. Greater visibility of carers is a consequence of their increasing status within tactics of government that have also brought greater levels of surveillance (Heaton, 1999; Henderson and Forbat, 2002) cementing forms of obligation distilled from this 'ethic' of care. Together these shifts contribute to the downgrading of holistic and ethical caring practice (Gregory and Holloway, 2005).

Example 2 of a Foucauldian Approach

Foucault (1977) views surveillance as a central technique that renders an individual the object of power/knowledge. Assessment practice, established in relation to normalized standards and roles as in this example, produces an intensification of chapterwork, protocolization, and the expansion of information and communication technologies. Hence, professionals also come under scrutiny as part of the continuous review of the client's needs a gaze that is 'always receptive' (Foucault 1977: 89) to managerial control catches all.

SOCIAL WORK AND POWER

The exercise of power, taken as the archetypal activity that defines professional practice, has provided the focus for a significant amount of debate and analysis concerning the status of professions in general and social work in particular. Discretion provides a paradoxical space for the operation of power both enticing resistance and inviting surveillance. The majority of this debate has focused on the way managerialism, managerial forms of supervision, and information technology has apparently undermined professional discretion (D'Cruz et al., 2009; Evans and Harris, 2004; Harris, 1998). Nevertheless, Evans and Harris (2004) provide an interesting discussion of discretion in social work practice drawing on Lipsky's (1980) work on 'street-level bureaucracy' which focused on face-to-face encounters of social workers with their clients. Analysis provides evidence that discretion is alive and well in social work practice although micro-politics of the context means that this has been subject to ongoing revision: again the dance of resistance and surveillance.

The spaces within which social workers 'translate nebulous policy into practical action' (Evans and Harris, 2004: 882) resonate with a Foucauldian analysis of governmentality and the persistence of professional authority in complex situations where actions cannot be pre-prescribed. Persistence of spaces between rules requires judgments by professionals over which 'rules' apply in contexts that contain multiple possibilities. Practitioners also use discretion when deciding to 'apply the rules' in this instance effectively closing down space. This leads to the proposition that discretion is a political activity that occurs in the context of uncertainty and complexity necessitating negotiation while highlighting localized and relational aspects of power.

This localized and relational aspect is also evident in power relations between practitioners and managers where enabling discretion has advantages for managers and organizations as it allows 'innovation' to be claimed for the organization when things work well while directing blame at front line practitioners when things go wrong, i.e., 'failed to follow procedures'. In addition, discretion allows managers to distance themselves from difficult day-to-day consequences of organizational goals such as gaps between actions and resources. Discretion therefore operates in spaces governed by uncertainty that involve bargaining and negotiation over responsibility (Evans and Harris, 2004). Indeed, networks of power relations operating via the most mundane interactions between managers, social workers, service users and carers enable the formation and shifting of alliances between political and non-political authorities where experts – professionals – and expertise are crucial to operations (D'Cruz et al., 2009; Parton, 1994). 'Micro-politics' is the localized context where policy decisions are given meaning through practical application and the identities of participants are produced in the reciprocal relations of power or 'performativity'. Performance is always relational, drawing others into the act: managers, other professionals, clients and so on constructing both meanings associated with performances and mutually dependent subject positions (Wetherell, 2001).

Such specific and localized contexts are typically complex with multiple demands providing circumstances where social workers can adopt different roles depending on their function and client group. There is always some degree of fluidity and uncertainty around expectations and therefore the space for discretion and thus innovation and resistance. In addition, social workers carry a range of discourses into these spaces. Face-to-face contact enables different forms of interaction from that characterized in routinized and objectified practice. It also allows social workers to 'reclaim the language' to re-establish holistic and ethical practice:

> Deconstructing the language of performance indicators and quality outcomes implies that rather than turning a conversation with a service user about how they think and feel about their situation into easily measurable service inputs, the social worker strives to reflect that conversation in the framing of objectives driven by the service user's internalized understanding of 'quality' (Gregory and Holloway, 2005: 50).

However, it is not sufficient to assume that all face-to-face encounters are in themselves holistic and ethical and by that alone avoid the oppressive nature of objectifying discourses and routinized practice. For example, discourses of anti-oppressive practice developed from a radical critique of social work causing the profession to reflect and review practice with major benefits at that

Example 2 of a Foucauldian Approach

time however; this discourse is now the nucleus of social work activity. Language and meaning associated with anti-racist and anti-oppressive practice are historically specific while discourse is dynamic allowing re-articulation of radical elements with more conservative positions that colonize and neutralize the discourse institutionalizing it in a range of organizational contexts:

> Indeed anti-oppressive practice has allowed the state to reposition itself as a benign arbiter between competing identity claims. Perversely, given its aim to make the personal political, it has allowed the problems of society to be recast as due to the moral failings of individuals who need censure and correction from the anti-oppressive social worker (McLaughlin, 2005: 300).

Similar contradictions arise in relation to the discourse of 'empowerment', which has become a theory of professional practice providing professionals with a central role in defining needs and designing interventions (Pease, 2002). Rose (1996) takes this criticism a stage further suggesting that discourses of empowerment translate as the 'role of experts in the coaxing of others who lack the cognitive, emotional, practical and ethical skills to take personal responsibility and engage in self-management'. Disciplinary techniques embedded in discourses of empowerment located in initiatives such as 'Sure Start' (UK Department of Health, 2003), 'community development projects', and public health projects (UK Department of Health, 2004), target 'damaged individuals' in an attempt to reform and normalize their conduct, encouraging them to take personal responsibility and engage in self-forming activities, self-care, and self-help (Jordan, 2000; Rose, 1999).

Nevertheless, a number of writers (Beresford, 2001; Butler, 2005; Evans and Harris, 2004; Gregory and Holloway, 2005; Harris, 1998; Hodge, 2005; Pease, 2002; Scheyett, 2006) emphasize, in different ways, social workers' potential for resistance in their practice with marginalized individuals and groups. Under such circumstances, social workers resist prevailing discourse defining individuals i.e. refugees and asylum seekers as a problem and undeserving. Instead, they provide space for the service users' to develop and express their perspective on needs and priorities. Here, discretion provides space for the renegotiation of events making resistance possible through the 'insurrection of subjugated knowledges' (Foucault 1977: 88).

However, such possibilities may already be constrained regardless of the values of individual social workers. Social workers' carry into their interactions 'icons' representing the collective experience of society concerning particular types of event (Kitzinger, 2000). These 'icons' are produced over time as a consequence of similar types of events e.g. child abuse cases, homicides perpetrated by users of mental health services, neglect and deaths of people subject to community care. Such events provoke intense media discussion while icons provide rhetorical shorthand for journalists and the public, which include interpretive frameworks that embed distortion and inaccuracy and provide templates for future events. As such, they have particular qualities; appear fixed and authoritative, and resist renegotiation. Discursively, they provide a backdrop for social work activity disciplining discretion through ghost-like media surveillance.

Surveillance in this world of face-to-face encounters takes more subtle forms than those produced by objectifying processes of routinized work, and information and communication technologies. Nevertheless, the dual aspect of bio-politics remains evident. At the macro-level, governance of professional activity requires professions to regulate the activity of practitioners by ensuring their commitment to professional development as a prerequisite to retaining a licence to practice. At the micro-level, discourse concerning the complexity of the social work task incites individual practitioners to adopt a position of reflexivity to their work (Taylor and White, 2000). Such reflexivity, achieved via confessional practices includes, among others, techniques of reflection and supervision (Gilbert, 2001; Rose, 1999). In turn, organizations require practitioners to engage in supervision as surveillance of individual practice thus promoting processes that enable managers to maintain 'the gaze' on individual social workers and the exercise of discretion in relation to their caseload. Managers themselves are also subject to supervision entangling all in an ever-extending web of surveillance.

Such subjectifying technologies operating alongside the objectifying technologies discussed earlier, exemplified by the use of information and communication technologies, reproduce the panopticon in a contemporary form no longer constrained by the physical limits of the hospital, school, prison, or barracks and enable the surveillance of social work activity across an increasingly complex and dispersed landscape. For Foucault (1977: 177), the panopticon integrates power and knowledge, the control of the 'body', and the control of space into a technology of discipline. To this, as noted earlier, we can also add a temporal dimension. It is efficient, since surveillance is everywhere and constant, and effective, because it is 'discreet', functioning 'permanently and in silence'. It also provides the scope for the supervision of those entrusted with the surveillance of others.

RESISTANCE AND SOCIAL WORK

Foucault (1977) wrote that where there is power, there is always resistance. White (2009) refers to actions such as these as examples of 'quiet resistance' and identifies the most common types as 'dressing up assessments' or strategic manipulation of knowledge and information about service users; bypassing decision-making procedures by deliberately delaying paperwork; overt cooperation with tasks which conceals resistance; 'resistance through distance' by escaping or avoiding managerial authority; cynicism; and withdrawal from active participation in the workplace, through sickness and stress, moving jobs, or leaving the profession. Such tactics are reminiscent of covert resistance adopted by subaltern groups throughout history as discussed by James C. Scott (2002) in his classic text *Domination and the Arts of Resistance,* where he refers to them as 'hidden transcripts' aimed at challenging the 'public transcripts' or official views and practices of dominant groups.

CRITIQUE OF FOUCAULT

While there is a strong claim for original insights to social work studies through the powerful work of Michel Foucault, there are several important questions that need to be raised, if the full complexity of the processes surrounding social work, social policy and power are to be appreciated and understood. There are points that need to be highlighted: critical pessimism; Foucault-Marxist duality; sociological structural fault lines and oppression.

First, one of the major criticisms centres on critical pessimism. As Powell and Chamberlain (2012: 158) suggest a Foucauldian approach does little to encourage or instruct anyone interested in undertaking such action. In addition, Foucault himself 'gives the impression that resistance is generally contained by power and poses no threat' (Powell and Chamberlain, 2012: 22)

Secondly, Foucault suggests subjectivity is not a fabricated part of a deeper reality but is itself an aspect of the reality systematically formulated by discourse and power relations. Foucault side-steps the binary relationship set up by Marxist theory between true and false realities, ways of knowing and political consciousness (Foucault, 1977). He loosens knowledge, ideas and subject positions from categories of social totality, such as social formation, mode of production, history, economy and society. Thus suspended from their ostensible connections, social ideas are re-articulated in Foucault's thought to historical and societal features ignored in Marxist models of social reality based on the labour process and modes of economic exploitation. Nevertheless, we can ask the question: is not the class structure a key determinant of the position of individuals in capitalist society? The implication is society itself makes it very difficult for 'resistance' when population groups are decommodified and lose social worth brought about by a loss of productive roles that puts premium on production. In addition, Foucault's notion of governmentality is problematic itself. A reflective critique is that Foucault failed to relate such 'arts of governmentality' to wider social class interests which may motivate policy development.

Thirdly, and coupled with the above, Foucault does not pay much particular attention to sociological fault lines of 'race', sexuality, disability, and gender and how they are blurred and splinter off from ageing as an discursive formation. What is not included in Foucault's work is how community groups collectively, in recent years, have formed and mobilised pressure groups to address power imbalances regarding adverse care assessment such as 'Grey Power'.

In conclusion, adopting a Foucauldian analysis enables a critical approach to the dynamics of knowledge and power that lays open the implications and possibilities of practices promoted by social policy and enacted by social workers. In addition, this perspective, by moving beyond conceptions of power as domination to consider power as relational poses a different range of questions over how particular subjects are formed, e.g., asylum seekers. Moreover, it raises questions over how that identity relates to the formation of other subjects on which subjectivity is dependent. Furthermore, exploring power as relational exposes many of the principles that have guided social work activity, such as empowerment and anti-oppressive to a critical stance, identifying how relations of power have seen such commitments detached from their original radical and humanitarian moorings to feature now as components of oppressive discourses they might once have challenged. Nevertheless, by identifying the effects of power as partial a Foucauldian perspective provides the possibility of resistance, enabling analysis of those many incidences, many mundane, some striking, where service users may come together with carers and social workers to establish alternatives to prevailing discourse and social practices. To contribute to this possibility social work is in need a of Foucauldian theory of power relations. Clarification takes place through an examination of the presuppositions that are embedded in world-views of social workers. However, these developments in social work have their shadow side, and the ethics of using such technologies to help clients such as older people through complex power relations have been subject to less scrutiny. Indeed, it is perhaps emblematic of contemporary Western culture that social work offers the promise of escape from, rather than a deepened understanding of identity.

Chapter 7

SUMMARY

In his essay on Kant's 'What is Enlightenment (*Was ist Aufklärung?*)?* Foucault writes of his work as being an 'historical ontology of ourselves' through a critique of what we do, say and think. He is clear throughout the essay concerning what this form of critique is not: neither a theory, doctrine, or body of knowledge that accumulates over time. Instead, it is an attitude, 'an ethos, a philosophical life in which the critique of what we are is at one and the same time the historical analysis of the limits that are imposed on us and an experiment with the possibility of going beyond them' (Foucault 1984: 50). What is the motivation for this work? 'How can the growth of capabilities be disconnected from the intensification of power relations?' (1984: 48).

There is no 'gesture of rejection' in this ethos. It moves beyond the 'Outside-inside alternative' in the name of a critique that 'consists of analyzing and reflecting upon limits' (Foucault 1984: 45). The purpose being 'to transform the critique conducted in the form of necessary limitation into a practical critique that takes the form of a possible transgression' (1984: 45). Overall, it is genealogical in form: 'it will not deduce from the form of what we are what it is impossible for us to do and to know; but it will separate out, from the contingency that has made us what we are, the possibility of no longer being, doing, or thinking what we are, do, or think' (1984: 46). The ideal lies in the possibility of setting oneself free. To examine the internal modes of the ordering of truth, but not in the name of a truth that lies beyond it, is seen to open up possibilities for its transgression.

Despite criticisms that his work lacked a normative dimension (Fraser 1989), the orientation for Foucault's approach is clear. The issue translates into one of how one-sided states of domination can be avoided in order to promote a two-sided relation of dialogue. Foucault's interventions were practically motivated. The journey for these investigations being from how we are constituted as objects of knowledge, to how we are constituted as subjects of power/knowledge. What we can take from Foucault is the insight that critical approaches to cultural analysis cannot practice on the presupposition that there is an essence to humanity. The idea of coming to know ourselves differently and viewing the possibilities for transformation, is about interpreting ourselves differently. Between self-definition and social situation lies the potential to render the 'cultural unconscious apparent' (Foucault 1989, 73).

REFERENCES

Armstrong, T. J (ed). (1992). *Michel Foucault: Philosopher.* Translated by Armstrong, T. J. London: Harvester Wheatsheaf.

Ashenden, S. and Owen, D. (eds) (1999). *Foucault Contra Habermas: Recasting the Dialogue between Genealogy and Critical Theory. London: Sage.*

Baines, D. (2004) 'Pro-market, Non-market: the Dual Nature of Organizational Change in Social Services Delivery' *Critical Social Policy* 24(1): 5-29.

Beck, U (1994) *The Risk Society,* London: Sage.

Beresford, P. (2001) Service users, social policy and the future of welfare. *Critical Social Policy* 21(4): 494 – 512.

Beresford, P., Croft, S., Evans, C. and Harding, T. (1997). Quality in personal social services: The developing role of user involvement in the U.K. In Evers, A., Haverinen, R., Leichsenring, K. and Winstow, G. (eds.) *Developing Quality in Personal Social Services: A European Perspective.* Aldershot: Ashgate pp 63 - 81.

Biggs, S. and Powell, J.L. (2000). Surveillance and Elder Abuse: The Rationalities and Technologies of Community Care, *Journal of Contemporary Health, 4, 1, pp.43-49.*

Biggs, S. and Powell, J.L. (2001). 'A Foucauldian Analysis of Old Age and the Power of Social Welfare', *Journal of Aging & Social Policy*, Vol.12, (2), pp.93-111.

Biggs, S. and Powell, J.L. (2001). 'A Foucauldian analysis of old age and the power of social welfare', *Journal of Aging & Social Policy* Vol.12, (2), 93-111.

Booth, T,. McConnell, D. and Booth, W. (2006). Temporal Discrimination and Parents with Learning Difficulties in the Child Protection System. *British Journal of Social Work,* 36(6): 997 – 1015.

Burchell, G., Gordon, C. and Miller, P. (eds) (1991). *The Foucault Effect: Studies in Governmentality.* London: Harvester Wheatsheaf.

Butler, A. (2005) A strengths approach to building bridges: UK students and refugees together. *Community Development Journal* 40(2): 147 – 157.

Butler, I. and Drakeford, M. (2001) 'Which Blair Project: Communitarianism, social authoritarianism and social work, *Journal of Social Work,* 1(1): 7 - 19.

Bytheway, W (1995) Ageism, Milton Keynes: OUP.

Chambon, A, S. (1999). Foucault's Approach, in Chambon, A, S., Irvine, A. and Epstein, L. [eds.] *Reading Foucault for Social Work.* New York, Columbia University Press.

Chau, W.F (1995) 'Experts, networks and inscriptions in the fabrication of accounting images', Accounting Organisations and Society, 20, 2/3, 111-145.

Clarke, J (1994) 'Capturing the Customer: Consumerism and Social Welfare', *paper to ESRC seminar Conceptualising Consumption Issues,* Dec.1994, University of Lancaster.

Clarke, J. and Newman, J. (1997) *The Managerial State,* London, Sage.

D'Cruz, H. Gillingham, P. and Melendez, S. (2009) Exploring the Possibilities of an Expanded Practice Repertoire in Child Protection. *Journal of Social Work,* 9(1): 61 – 85.

Davidson, A. (1986). 'Archaeology, Genealogy, Ethics' in Hoy, D (Ed.*)* *Foucault: a critical reader,* Oxford: Basil Blackwell.

Dean, M. (1994). A social structure of many souls: Moral regulation, government, and self-formation. *Canadian Journal of Sociology.* 19(2), 145-168.

Dean, M. (2007). *Governing Societies.* Maidenhead: Open University Press/McGraw-Hill.

Deleuze, G. (1992). '*What is* a dispositif?'. In Armstrong, T. J. (ed).

Department of Health (2005a). *Choosing Health: Making Health Choices Easier Cm 6374.* London: The Stationery Office.

Department of Health [DH] (2002). *Implementing the Caldicott Standard into Social Care. HSC 2002/003:LCA (2002/2,* London: Department of Health.

Department of Health [DH] (2003). *Every Child Matters* Cm 5860. London: The Stationery Office.

References 57

Department of Health [DH] (2005b). Independence, Well-being and Choice Cm 6499. London: The Stationery Office.

Department of Health [DH] (2006) Our Health, Our Care, Our Say: A new direction for community services CM 6737, London: The Stationery Office.

Department of Health and Social Security [DHSS] (1990). *The National Health Service and Community Care Act.* London: The Stationery Office.

Department of Health, Department for Education and Employment, Home Office [DH/DfEE/HO] (2000), *Framework for the Assessment of Children in Need and their Families.* London: The Stationery Office.

Donzelot, J. (1980). *The Policing of Families.*

Dreyfus, H, L. and Rabinow, P. (1982). *Michel Foucault: Beyond Structuralism and Hermeneutics.* Brighton: Harvester.

Dreyfus, H. and Rabinow, P. (1982). *Michel Foucault: Beyond Structuralism and Hermeneutics.* Chicago: University of Chicago Press.

Dyer, J. and Keller-Cohen, D. (2000). The discursive construction of professional self through narratives of personal experience. *Discourse Studies,* 2(3): 283 – 304.

Elders, F. (ed) (1974). *Reflexive Waters: The Basic Concerns of Mankind.* London: Souvenir Press.

Engels, F and Marx, K (1985) The Communist Manifesto.

Estes, C (1979) The Aging Enterprise, San Francisco: Jossey Bass.

Evans, T. and Harris, J. (2004). Street-Level Bureaucracy, Social Work and the (Exaggerated) Death of Discretion. *British journal of Social Work,* 34: 871 - 895.

Fleming, P. (2005) Metaphors of Resistance, *Management Communication Quarterly,* 19(1): 45 – 66.

Foucault, M (1967) Madness and Civilisation, London: Tavistock.

Foucault, M (1972) The Archaeology of Knowledge, London: Tavistock.

Foucault, M (1973) The Birth of the Clinic, London: Routledge.

Foucault, M (1976) The History of Sexuality, Harmandsworth: Penguin.

Foucault, M (1977) Discipline and Punish, London: Tavistock.

Foucault, M (1980) Power/Knowledge: Selected Interviews and Other Writings, 1972-1977, New York: Pantheon.

Foucault, M (1982) 'The subject of Power' in Dreyfus, H and Rabinow, P (Eds.) Michel Foucault: beyond structuralism and hermeneutics, Brighton: Harvester.

Foucault, M (1984) 'What is Enlightenment?' in Rabinow, P (Ed.) The Foucault Reader, London: Peregrine.

Foucault, M. (1984). *The Foucault Reader.* Edited by Rabinow, P. Harmondsworth: Penguin.

Foucault, M. (1989). *Foucault Live: Collected Interviews 1961-1984.* Edited by Lotringer, E. Translated by Johnston, J. New York: Semiotext(e).

Foucault, M. (1991a). *Remarks on Marx: Conversations with Duccio Trombadori.* Translated by Goldstein, R. J. and Cascaito, J. New York: Semiotext(e).

Foucault, M. (1991b). 'The Ethic of Care for the Self as a Practice of Freedom: An interview with Fornet-Betancourt, R., Becker, H. and Gomez-Müller, A. Translated by Gauthier Snr, J. D. In Bernauer, J. and Rasmussen, D. (eds). *The Final Foucault.* Massachusetts: MIT Press.

Foucault, M. (1997). *Ethics: Subjectivity and Truth. The Essential Works, Volume 1.* Edited by Rabinow, P. Translated by Hurley, R et al. London: Allen Lane, The Penguin Press.

Foucault, M. (1967). *Madness and Civilisation.* London: Tavistock.

Foucault, M. (1972). *The Archaeology of Knowledge.* London: Tavistock.

Foucault, M. (1973). *The Birth of the Clinic.* London: Routledge.

Foucault, M. (1976). *The History of Sexuality.* Harmondsworth: Penguin.

Foucault, M. (1977) *Discipline and Punish.* London, Allen Lane.

Foucault, M. (1977). *Discipline and Punish.* London: Tavistock.

Foucault, M. (1978). 'Governmentality' in Burchell, G. (ed.). (1991*). The Foucault Effect: Studies in Governmentality.* Wheatsheaf: Harvester.

Foucault, M. (1978). The History of Sexuality [Volume 1]: An Introduction. New York, Vintage Books.

Foucault, M. (1980). *Power/Knowledge: Selected Interviews and Other Writings, 1972-1977,* Edited by Gordon, C. New York: Pantheon.

Foucault, M. (1983). 'The subject of Power' in Dreyfus, H. and Rabinow, P. (Eds.) *Michel Foucault: beyond structuralism and hermeneutics.* Brighton: Harvester.

Foucault, M. (1988). *'Technologies of the Self' in Martin, L.H. et al. (Eds.).* Technologies of the Self. *London: Tavistock.*

Fournier, V. (1999) 'The Appeal to `Professionalism' as a Disciplinary Mechanism', *The Sociological Review* 47 (2), pp. 280-307.

Fournier, V. (2000) Boundary work and the (un-) making of the professions, in N. Malin (ed.) *Professionalism, Boundaries and the Workplace* , London, Routledge, pp. 67-86.

Fournier, V. (2001) 'Amateurism, Quackery and Professional Conduct: the constitution of 'proper' aromatherapy practice', in M. Dent and S. Whitehead (eds.) *Managing professional identities: knowledge,*

References

performativities and the 'new' professional. London: Routledge, pp. 116-137.

Freenberg, A. (1991). *Critical theory of technology*. New York, Oxford University Press.

Garland, D. (1985). *Punishment and Welfare*. Aldershot: Gower.

Garrett, P, M. (2002) Encounters in the new welfare domains of the third way: Social Work, the Connexions agency and personal advisors. *Critical Social Policy* 22(4): 596 - 618.

Garrett, P, M. (2003). Swimming with Dolphins: The Assessment Framework, New Labour and New Tools for Social Work with Children and Families. *British Journal of Social Work,* 33(4): 441 - 463.

Garrett, P, M. (2005) Social Work's 'electronic turn': notes on the deployment of information and communication technologies in social work with children and families. *Critical Social Policy* 25(4): 529 – 553.

Giddens, A (1991) The Consequences of Modernity, Cambridge: Polity.

Gilbert T. (2001) Reflective practice and clinical supervision: meticulous rituals of the confessional. *Journal of Advanced Nursing* 36(2) 199-205.

Gilbert, T and Powell, J.L. (2005) 'Family, Caring and Aging in the UK', *Scandinavian Journal of Caring Sciences*, 41, 2, 41-48.

Gordon, C (1980) [ed.]. *Michel Foucault: Power/Knowledge: Selected interviews and other writings 1972 – 1977.* London: Harvester Wheatsheaf.

Gregory, M., and Holloway, M. (2005) Language and the Shaping of Social Work. *British Journal of Social Work,* 35(1): 37 - 5.

Grey, C. (1998) 'On Being A Professional In A 'Big Six' Firm', *Accounting, Organizations and Society* 23 (5-6) pp. 569-587.

Harris, J. (1998) Scientific Management, bureau-professionalism, new managerialism: The labour process of state social work. *British Journal of Social Work,* 28(6): 839 - 862.

Harris, J. (2002) Caring for Citizenship. *British Journal of Social Work* 32(3): 267- 281.

Heaton, J. (1999). The Gaze and the Viability of the Carer: A Foucauldian Analysis of the Discourse of Informal Care. *Sociology of Health and Illness,* 21(6): 759 – 777.

Heffernan, K (2006). Social Work, New Public Management and the Language of 'Service User'. *British Journal of Social Work,* 36(1): 139 - 147.

Henderson, J. and Forbat, L. (2002) Relationship-based social policy: personal and policy constructions of 'care'. *Critical Social Policy,* 22(4): 669 – 687.

HM Government (2007). *Putting People First: a shared vision and commitment to the transformation of adult social care.* London: TSO.

Hochschild, A.R. (1983) *The Managed Heart: The Commercialization of Human Feeling* London, University of California Press.

Hodge, S (2005). Participation, discourse and power: a case study in service user involvement. *Critical Social Policy*, 25(2): 164 - 179.

Hudson, J. (2000a). 'E-galitarianism? The information society and New Labour's Repositioning of Welfare'. *Critical Social Policy,* 23(2): 268 – 291.

Hudson, J. (2002b). 'Digitalising the structures of government: the UK's Information Age Government Agenda. *Policy and Politics,* 30(4): 268515 – 531.

Hugman, R (1991) *Power in Caring Professions* Hampshire, Macmillan.

Johnson, T (2001) Governmentality and the institutionalization of expertise, in M Purdy and D Banks [eds.], *The Sociology and Politics of Health: A Reader.* London: Routledge pp 135-143.

Johnson, T.J. (1972) *Professions and Power.* London, Macmillan.

Jones, C. (2001) 'Voices from the Front-Line: State Social Workers and New Labour' *British Journal of Social Work* 31(4): 547-562.

Jordan, B, (1989) *The Common Good: Citizenship, Morality and self-Interest.* Oxford: Basil Blackwell.

Jordan, B. with Jordan, C. (2000) *Social Work and the Third Way: Tough love as social policy.* London, Sage.

Jordon, B. (2005) New Labour: Choice and values. *Critical Social Policy,* 25(4): 427 - 446.

Katz, S (1996) Disciplining Old Age: The formation of gerontological knowledge, Charlottesville: University of Virginia.

Keenan, E, K. (2001). Using Foucault's 'Disciplinary Power' and 'Resistance' in Cross-Cultural Psychotherapy. *Clinical Social Work Journal,* 29(3): 211- 226.

Kendall, G and Wickham, G. (1999) *Using Foucault's Methods.* London: Sage.

Kitzinger, J. (2000). Media templates: patterns of association and the (re)construction of meaning over time. *Media, Culture and Society,* 22(1) 66 - 84.

References 61

Knights, D. and McCabe, C. (2003). *Innovation and Organisation: Guru Schemes and American Dreams.* Maidenhead: Open University Press/McGraw-Hill.

Laming, H. Lord (2009) *The Protection of Children in England: A Progress Report.* London: TSO.

Lewis, J. and Glennerster, H. (1996*) Implementing the New Community Care* Milton Keynes, Open University Press.

Lipsky, M. (1980). *Street-level Bureaucracy: The dilemmas of individuals in public services.* New York: Russell Sage Foundation.

Marx, K and Engels, F (1985) The Communist Manifesto, London: Verso.

May, T. (1991). Probation: Politics, Policy and Practice. Milton Keynes: Open University Press.

May, T. (1994). 'Transformative Power: A Study in a Human Service Organisation'. *Sociological Review.* Vol 42 (4). pp. 618-638.

May, T. (1999). 'From Banana Time to Just-in-Time: Power and Resistance at Work'. *Sociology.* Vol 33 (4). pp. 767-783.

McLaughlin, K. (2005) From ridicule to institutionalization: anti-oppression, the state and social work. *Critical Social Policy*, 25(3): 283 - 305.

McNay, L. (1994) *Foucault.* Polity: Cambridge.

Merquior, J (1985) Michel Foucault, New York: Fontana.

Miller, T. (1993). *The Well-Tempered Self: Citizenship, Culture and the Postmodern Subject.* Baltimore: John Hopkins University Press.

Monroe, E. (2004). The Impact of Audit on Social Work Practice. *British Journal of Social Work,* 34(8): 1075 - 1095.

Nettleton, S. (1997). Governing the risky self: how to become healthy, wealthy and wise, in Petersen, A. and Bunton, R. (eds.) *Foucault: Health and Medicine.* London: Routledge.

Osborne, T. (1997). Of health and statecraft, in Petersen, A. and Bunton, R. (eds.) *Foucault: Health and Medicine.* London: Routledge.

Owen, D. (1997). *Maturity and Modernity: Nietzsche, Weber, Foucault and the Ambivalence of Reason.* London: Routledge.

Parrot, L. and Madoc-Jones, I. (2008) Reclaiming Information and communication Technologies for Empowering Social Work Practice. *Journal of Social Work*, 8(2): 181 – 197.

Parton, N. (1994), 'Problematics of Government', (Post) Modernity and Social Work, *British Journal of Social Work,* 24(9): 9 - 32.

Pease, B. (2002). Rethinking Empowerment: A Postmodern Reappraisal for Emancipatory Practice. *British Journal of Social Work,* 32(2): 135 - 147.

Phillipson, C and Walker, A (Eds.) (1986) Ageing and Social Policy: A Critical Assessment, Aldershot: Gower.

Pithouse, A. (1998) *Social Work: The Social Organization of an Invisible Trade, 2nd edition,* Aldershot, Ashgate.

Postle, K. (2001) 'The Social Work Side Is Disappearing. I Guess It Started With Us Being Called Care Managers' *Practice* 13 (1): 3-18.

Powell, J (1998a) review of Katz, S (1996) 'Disciplining Old Age: The formation of gerontological knowledge' in Acta Sociologica, Vol. 41, No. 4, pp. 398-99.

Powell, J (1998b) 'The Us and The Them: Connecting Foucauldian and Political Economy insights into ageing bodies', unpublished paper presented British Sociological Association's Annual Conference, University of Edinburgh.

Powell, J and Chamberlain, M (2012) *Social Welfare, Aging and Social Theory,* New York, Lexington.

Powell, J.L (2001) 'The NHS and Community Care Act (1990) in the UK: A Critical Review', *Sincronia: Journal of Social Sciences and Humanities,* 5, (3), 1-10.

Powell, J.L and Biggs, S. (2000) 'Managing Old Age: The Disciplinary Web of Power Surveillance and Normalization', *Journal of Aging & Identity,* 5 (1), 3-13.

Rabinow, P (Ed.) (1984) The Foucault Reader, London: Peregrine.

Richardson, S. and Asthana, S (2006). Inter-agency information sharing in health and social care services: the role of professional culture. *British Journal of Social Work,* 36(4): 657 - 669.

Rose N (1999). *Powers of Freedom: Reframing political thought.* Cambridge: Cambridge University Press.

Rose, N and Miller, P (1992) 'Political Power Beyond the State: Problematics of Government', *The British Journal of Sociology,* 43, (2), 172-205.

Rose, N. (1993). Government, authority and expertise in advanced liberalism. *Economy and Society.* August. 22(3). 283-299.

Rose, N. (1996). The death of the social? Re-figuring the territory of government. *Economy and Society.* 25(3), 327-356.

Salvo, M, J. (2004) Rhetorical Action in Professional space: Information Architecture as Critical Practice. *Journal of Business and Technical Communication,* 18(1) 39 – 66.

Scheyett, A. (2006) Silence and Surveillance: Mental Illness, Evidence –Based practice, and a Foucualtian Lens. *Journal of Progressive Human Sciences,* 17(1): 71 – 92.

References 63

Seebohm Report (1968) *Report of the Committee on local authority and allied personal social Services,* Cmnd 3703. London: HMSO.

Selwyn, N. (2002). 'E-stablishing' an Inclusive Society? Technology, Social Exclusion and UK Government Policy Making. *Journal of social Policy,* 31(1): 1 - 20.

Sheppard, M. (1995). *Care Management and the New Social Work.* London: Whiting and Birch.

Shumway, D (1989) Michel Foucault, Charlottesville: University Press of Virginia.

Smart, B (1985) Michel Foucault, London: Routledge.

Smart, B. (1983*). Foucault, Marxism and Critique.* London: Routledge and Kegan Paul.

Stott, M (1981) Ageing for Beginners, Oxford: Blackwell.

Taylor, C. and White, S. (2000). *Practicing Reflexivity in Health and Social Care: Making Knowledge.* Buckingham: Open University Press.

Tew, J. (2006) Understanding Power and Powerlessness: Towards a Framework for Emancipatory Practice in Social Work. *Journal of Social Work,* 6(1): 33 - 51.

Tilbury, C. (2004). The Influence of Performance Measurement on Child welfare Policy and Practice. *British Journal of Social Work,* 34(2): 225 – 241.

Turner, B, S. (1997). From governmentality to risk: Some reflections on Foucault's contribution to medical sociology, in Petersen, A. and Bunton, R. (eds.) *Foucault: Health and Medicine.* London: Routledge pp ix – xxii.

Warnes, A (Ed.) (1996) Human Ageing and Later Life, London: Edward Arnold.

Wetherell, M. (2001) Themes in Discourse Research: The Case of Diana, in Wetherell, M., Taylor, S., &Yates, S, J., [eds.] *Discourse Theory and Practice*, London: Sage pp 14 – 28.

Whitehead, S., (1998) Disrupted Selves: resistance and identity work in the managerial arena, *Gender and Education*, 10(2): 199 - 215.

INDEX

#

20th century, 1

A

abuse, 31
access, 39, 41
accountability, 36, 40, 43
accounting, 56
administrators, 14, 36
adults, 38, 39
age, 27, 28
ageing population, 14, 37
agencies, 42
aging population, 32
AIDS, 1
American Psychiatric Association, 44
anatomy, 32
antagonism, 15
articulation, 47
assessment, 28, 29, 30, 31, 34, 38, 39, 42, 43, 44, 50
assessment tools, 42
asylum, 47, 50
attitudes, 6, 28
audit, 11, 39, 41, 42, 43
Australasia, 23, 24
authoritarianism, 56

authority(s), 5, 10, 11, 14, 17, 36, 37, 40, 45, 46, 49, 62, 63
autonomy, 23, 28, 40, 41, 44
awareness, 1

B

bargaining, 46
benefits, 46
benign, 47
blame, 43, 46
bureaucracy, 45

C

capitalism, 9
case study, 60
catalyst, 14
causality, 2
challenges, 24, 34
charities, 36
chemical, 14
Chicago, 57
child abuse, 43, 48
child protection, 43
children, 14, 38, 39, 59
circulation, 12, 26
citizens, 37
citizenship, 37
class struggle, 19

classification, 9, 11, 14, 24, 31, 35
clients, 30, 33, 40, 41, 43, 44, 45, 46, 51
climate, 30
coercion, 18
coherence, 34
communication, 39, 41, 42, 45, 48, 59, 61
communication technologies, 39, 41, 45, 48, 59
community(s), 34, 43, 47, 48, 50, 57
community service, 57
competition, 36
complexity, 18, 37, 45, 48, 49
conception, 43
configuration, 5, 18
conflict, 34
conformity, 15, 17
consciousness, 19, 23, 49
consensus, 30, 37
consolidation, 23, 24
construction, 10, 18, 28, 37, 57, 60
consumers, 28
contextual backdrops, 3
contingency, 18, 53
controversial, 1, 14, 37
cooperation, 49
cost, 43
counterbalance, 40
covering, 38
criminality, 17, 23, 25
criticism, 47
cultural practices, 2
culture, 18, 19, 20, 25, 43, 51, 62

D

dance, 33, 35, 40, 45
deaths, 48
decay, 27
depth, 12
Diagnostic and Statistical Manual of Mental Disorders, 44
disability, 50
discrimination, 43
discursive formations, 3
diseases, 27

distribution, 3, 26, 31, 33, 44
distribution of power, 3, 33
doctors, 26
dominance, 28
drawing, 35, 45, 46
dream, 18
DSM-IV-TR, 44
duality, 49

E

economic fluctuation, 9
education, 38
elderly population, 31
empowerment, 28, 47, 50
energy, 28
England, 38, 43, 61
environment, 43
ethics, 18, 51
everyday life, 20, 27
evidence, 28, 35, 44, 45
evil, 20
exclusion, 20
execution, 29
exercise, 1, 12, 13, 20, 28, 35, 40, 41, 42, 45, 48
expertise, 15, 36, 41, 46, 60, 62
exploitation, 20, 50

F

fabrication, 56
factories, 29
faith, 28
families, 36, 39, 43, 59
family support, 43
financial, 28, 30, 31
financial resources, 31
food, 12
force, 19
formation, 5, 10, 14, 20, 35, 36, 37, 46, 49, 50, 56, 60, 62
formula, 38
framing, 46

Index 67

France, 1
freedom, 20, 41
friendship, 13

G

gender inequality, 13
general practitioner, 24
gestures, 6, 26
governance, 48
governments, 11, 37
governor, 40
grids, 14
growth, 53
guidelines, 43

H

happiness, 11, 17
health, 14, 27, 28, 33, 37, 38, 40, 41, 44, 61, 62
hermeneutics, 57, 58
history, 5, 7, 10, 13, 14, 15, 17, 49
HM, 38, 60
homogeneity, 30
human, 9, 10, 11, 12, 13, 14, 15, 19, 20, 36
human agency, 15
human body, 12, 13, 36
human experience, 12
human sciences, 9, 12

I

ideal, 53
identification, 35, 43
identity, 15, 19, 24, 27, 33, 36, 47, 50, 63
image(s), 44, 56
imbalances, 50
immortality, 17
imprisonment, 28, 32
inattention, 6
indecency, 6
Independence, 38, 57
individuality, 11, 27, 31

individuals, 1, 2, 11, 12, 14, 15, 17, 18, 19, 27, 29, 31, 34, 35, 37, 38, 47, 50, 61
induction, 40
industry, 12
information sharing, 62
information technology, 45
infrastructure, 44
inmates, 5, 23, 26
insertion, 26, 44
institutions, 1, 2, 5, 9, 11, 14, 19, 28, 37, 38
intellectual disabilities, 43
interdependence, 18
intermittent observation, 2
intervention, 9, 13, 18, 27, 36
isolation, 18
issues, vii, 17, 19, 25, 30, 31, 41

J

Jordan, 37, 47, 60
journalists, 48

K

Keynes, 56, 61

L

landscape, 48
lead, 39
learning, 18
legislation, 41
lens, 37
liberalism, 62
liberation, 15
liberty, 11
light, 12, 14
local government, 28
love, 60

M

machinery, 32

68 Index

majority, 45
management, 7, 14, 23, 24, 25, 28, 30, 33, 34, 36, 37, 38, 40, 41, 42, 47
manipulation, 13, 18, 36, 49
Marx, 57, 58, 61
materials, 12
matrix, 14
matter, 25
measurement(s), 24, 31
media, 48
medical, 19, 27, 28, 31, 63
medicine, 11, 17, 20, 24, 25, 26, 27, 28, 39
mental health, 44, 48
mental illness, vii
methodology, 6, 7
mixed economy, 24, 28
models, 20, 24, 28, 40, 50
modern society, vii, 26, 44
modernity, 2, 9, 11, 12, 14, 20, 36
momentum, 24
monopoly, 34
moral imperative, 14, 37
morality, 7
motivation, 53

N

narratives, 11, 18, 57
National Health Service, 57
negative consequences, 43
neglect, 6, 7, 48
negotiation, 45, 46
NHS, 62
Nietzsche, 6, 61
North America, 37
nucleus, 47

O

objectification, 14, 35, 36
offenders, 11, 29
old age, 27, 28, 30, 55
operations, 11, 17, 46
opportunities, 39

oppression, 49, 61

P

parents, 43
participants, 46
performance indicator, 43, 46
permeation, 27
permit, 11
personal responsibility, 47
pessimism, 49
pharmaceutical, 19
playing, 34
police, 14, 37
policy, 23, 24, 38, 39, 42, 43, 44, 45, 46, 50, 60
policy makers, 42
political affiliations, 36
political power, 39
political problems, 11
politics, 10, 13, 19, 20, 34, 36, 38, 39, 42, 45, 46, 48
population, 12, 13, 14, 15, 24, 34, 36, 37, 38, 50
population control, 14, 36
population group, 50
power relations, 12, 13, 14, 15, 20, 25, 26, 28, 30, 34, 37, 39, 40, 44, 45, 49, 50, 53
pressure groups, 50
prestige, 39
principles, 50
prisoners, 14, 23, 24, 25, 26, 27, 28, 29, 30, 31
prisons, 5, 11, 12, 24, 25, 29, 31
private sector, 42
probe, 24, 26, 29, 31
professional development, 48
professionalism, 40, 59
professionalization, 40
professionals, 33, 34, 35, 36, 40, 41, 42, 45, 46, 47
project, 1, 6, 27, 37
proposition, 18, 45
protection, 41
psychiatry, 7, 17, 24

Index

69

psychoanalysis, 11
psychology, 11
public health, 47
public sector, 42
public service, 61
punishment, 24, 25, 28, 29, 30
purity, 11, 17

Q

questioning, 10, 17

R

race, 19, 50
rationality, 12, 14
reality, 19, 49
recognition, 25, 26
reconstruction, 10
reflective practice, 40
reflexivity, 28, 48
reform(s), 23, 47
refugees, 47, 56
regulations, 14, 37
rehabilitation, 6
rejection, 12, 53
relevance, vii, 9, 24, 25, 26, 28, 33, 44
reproduction, 25
requirements, 27
resistance, 13, 14, 19, 20, 21, 34, 35, 37, 40,
   41, 42, 45, 46, 47, 49, 50, 63
resource allocation, 30
resources, 26, 46
response, 39
restructuring, 37
rhetoric, 42
rights, 6, 11, 31, 44
risk(s), 24, 28, 31, 37, 39, 43, 63
risk assessment, 24, 39
routines, 29
rules, 5, 10, 33, 40, 45

S

school, 11, 12, 29, 36, 38, 48
science, 7, 11, 27, 28, 30, 41
scope, 29, 48
security, 9
self-control, 17
self-definition, 54
self-discipline, 41
self-knowledge, 35
self-regulation, 38
self-understanding, 17
sensitivity, 13
services, 30, 31, 37, 38, 42, 43, 44, 48, 62
sexual identity, 11
sexuality, 2, 6, 11, 13, 17, 20, 25, 28, 50
shape, 3, 28, 29, 41
signs, 19, 27
social behaviour(s), 2
social care, 38, 39, 41, 60, 62
social class, 50
social construct, 26
social context, 34, 38
social contract, 23
social group, 20
social institutions, 25, 36, 38
social life, 6, 18, 34
social network, 34
social order, 11
social phenomena, 2
social policy, 33, 36, 44, 49, 50, 55, 60
social problems, 14, 36
social reality, 20, 50
social reformer, 2
social regulation, 10, 24, 28
social relations, 12, 13, 18, 24, 35
social relationships, 13, 24, 35
social sciences, 9
Social Security, 57
social services, 38, 39, 41, 55
social structure, 19, 56
social theory, vii, 5
social welfare, 33, 37, 40, 42, 55
social work practitioners, 41

social workers, 33, 37, 38, 39, 40, 41, 42, 43, 45, 46, 47, 48, 50
society, vii, 1, 2, 6, 9, 10, 12, 19, 26, 27, 30, 33, 47, 49, 60
sociology, 14, 63
software, 42
solitude, 10
solution, 24
specialization, 39
species, 13, 36
specific knowledge, 35
speech, 6
spending, 30
standardization, 43
state(s), 2, 11, 13, 14, 17, 18, 24, 28, 36, 37, 47, 53, 59, 61
statistics, 14, 37
stereotypes, 40
storage, 6
stress, 49
structuralism, 19, 57, 58
structure, 6, 9, 11, 19, 25, 50
structuring, 36, 39
subjectivity, vii, 3, 9, 10, 12, 14, 18, 19, 25, 34, 40, 49, 50
supernatural, 11
supervision, 29, 31, 40, 41, 45, 48, 59
supervisors, 30
surveillance, 2, 10, 11, 13, 15, 21, 24, 25, 26, 27, 28, 29, 30, 31, 35, 37, 39, 41, 42, 43, 44, 45, 48
symptoms, 27
synthesis, 15

T

tactics, 1, 7, 15, 19, 40, 44, 49
target, 47
teachers, 24
techniques, 9, 10, 11, 12, 13, 19, 24, 25, 28, 31, 33, 34, 35, 47, 48
technology(s), 2, 11, 12, 14, 17, 18, 19, 24, 25, 26, 29, 33, 34, 35, 40, 41, 42, 43, 44, 48, 51, 59

tension, 41
territory, 36, 62
thoughts, 10, 17
torture, 29
trade, 36
trade union, 36
training, 11, 39
transcripts, 49
transformation, 5, 13, 18, 23, 36, 54, 60
transgression, 53
treatment, 27, 28

U

United Kingdom (UK), ii, 23, 24, 37, 38, 41, 43, 47, 56, 59, 60, 62, 63
United, 23, 37
universities, 38
USA, 23, 24, 44

V

variations, 30
vein, 43, 44
victims, 14
vision(s), 1, 2, 12, 20, 60

W

war, 15, 19, 30
web, 7, 25, 35, 48
welfare, 14, 20, 23, 28, 30, 33, 37, 39, 40, 43, 55, 59, 63
welfare system, 33, 40
well-being, 38
withdrawal, 49
work activity, 41, 43, 47, 48, 50
workers, 23, 34, 37, 39, 42, 44, 46, 47, 50
workplace, 49
World War I, 1